# Stick Figure

## A Diary of My Former Self

# Lori Gottlieb

Simon & Schuster
New York   London   Sydney   Singapore

SIMON & SCHUSTER
Rockefeller Center
1230 Avenue of the Americas
New York, NY 10020

Designed by Karolina Harris
Manufactured in the United States of America
10 9 8 7 6 5 4 3 2 1
Library of Congress Cataloging-in-Publication Data
Gottlieb, Lori.
    Stick figure : a diary of my former self / Lori Gottlieb.
        p. cm.
    1. Gottlieb, Lori—Health. 2. Anorexia nervosa—Patients—Biogra-
phy. I. Title.

RC552.A5 G68 2000
616.85'263'0092—dc21
[B]
                                                          99-052226
ISBN 0-684-86358-8

AUTHOR'S NOTE: This is a work of nonfiction. The names and identities
of people, excluding members of my immediate family and certain well-
known entertainment figures, have been changed to protect their
anonymity. The book is based on diaries I kept over a one-year period.
Some liberties have been taken with chronology.

Today's my half birthday. It's the first day of summer, and I'm exactly eleven and a half. I usually make a wish on my half birthdays, so I was thinking that I'd wish to be the thinnest girl at school, or maybe even the thinnest eleven-year-old on the entire planet. . . . I was just about to make the wish, but I sort of wondered what I'll have left to wish for on my real birthday, if I finally get that thin. I mean, what are girls supposed to wish for, other than being thin?

— June 1978

# Contents

# One Year Diary

Name: Lori Gottlieb

Age: 11

Gift From: Mom

Year: 1978

# 1:
## Winter 1978

# "Who Do You Think You Are, Young Lady?"

First of all, I should probably tell you about me and school and stuff, so you'll get what I'm talking about when I write in you. I mean, I *know* you're not a real person, but I still feel like you'll get me. More than people maybe. That's because people think I'm different. They usually call me "unique," which, depending on how you say it, could mean that I'm interesting or special or something. Like I stand out in a good way. But with me it never does. The truth is, everyone who calls me unique thinks I'm a complete weirdo. *Especially* adults.

I have to talk to adults a lot because Mom and Dad always have their boring friends over for cocktails before they go out to dinner, which means that me and David—that's my older brother—have to brush our hair and come downstairs and smile and act polite. David's pretty good at talking to adults, mostly because he can keep smiling the whole time he's telling them how great school and skateboarding are. I tried, I really did, but I just can't smile and talk at the same time. Especially if I'm talking about something sad—like how the sun's gonna burn us all to death because ladies use too much hair spray. It's true. It said so in a magazine.

So whenever I'm trying to talk to adults, they start nodding their heads up and down like they aren't even listening. Then right when I get to the important part—like how it'll only take a few seconds for our entire bodies to fry—their nods switch from up and down to side to side. That's when their eyes get really wide and they turn to my parents and say, "She's such a *unique* little girl." I always feel like saying, "Or maybe you're just incredibly *boring*," but I never do. Adults hate it when you have opinions about things.

Anyway, the whole reason you're here in the first place is because I was reading *The Diary of Anne Frank* last week over Christmas vacation. It took me two days, and I cried my head off. Anne thought about a lot of the same things I think about, but no one went around calling *her* unique. Not once. I couldn't stop thinking about Anne the whole week, even when I went shopping with Mom today. We were at this store in Beverly Hills where they have all kinds of expensive but tacky stuff that Mom gets a big kick out of. That's where I saw these fancy diaries with fake gold trim that you could give as gifts. You're one of them. No offense or anything.

Mom had the store lady put bright pink decorations on your cover, which looks kind of like lipstick. One thing you should know right away about Mom is that she's madly in love with lipstick. Everywhere she goes, Mom carries around this big purse full of makeup, just in case she suddenly feels like putting more on. I'm not too into makeup because you always have to be careful that you don't blink too much, or laugh too hard, or scratch your cheeks if they itch, or eat anything that might smudge your gloss. It's a pain in the butt, if you want my opinion. But all of my friends are starting to get curious about makeup, so now even Mom thinks I'm unique because I couldn't care less about the whole thing.

I don't know, sometimes I wonder if maybe I *am* unique. I mean, I used to be pretty normal, but things are different now that I'm eleven. I know it sounds conceited to say, but when I was in first grade I was really popular. I was best friends with

Leslie and Lana, and everyone called us "the three L's" because we always played together at recess. Except then in second grade, Leslie and Lana ended up in the same homeroom class with all my other friends, and I ended up in Mrs. Collins's class with no one I knew. Someone said that Mrs. Collins's class had all the smart kids in it, but the school said they couldn't "confirm or deny" that. A lot of kids' dads are lawyers, so my school's always afraid of getting sued. At least that's what Uncle Bob said, and he's a lawyer.

So that's when all the trouble started. First of all, my long blond hair kept getting darker and darker until it finally turned brown. I know it doesn't sound that terrible, but one of Mom's magazines said if you have "dishwater brown" hair, you should take that "boring" hair and make it more "exciting" by dyeing it red or platinum blond. Then next to the article there were these pictures of three different ladies with brown, red, and blond hair. The redhead and the blond lady were smiling like those people on game shows who win trips to Hawaii, but the lady with the brown hair looked like she was about to cry. So now I'm stuck with hair that makes you cry. But that's just part of what's happened to me since second grade. Believe me, it gets a *hundred* times worse.

You see, the whole time my hair was turning brown, the school kept sending me down to see Miss Shaw, our guidance counselor. I usually liked going to see Miss Shaw because she made me do fun puzzles and story games all the time. She never told me that the games were really IQ tests. But then this year she brought my parents in for a conference and told us that my IQ was like a high school kid's. She said if I didn't want to be so bored in class, maybe I should skip a grade or two. All the teachers at my school think I cause trouble because I like to do my own assignments instead of theirs. I'll bet my English teacher, Mrs. Rivers, wanted me to skip ahead so I wouldn't bug her so much, but Miss Shaw didn't say that, probably because she could get sued. I'm telling you, Mrs. Rivers hates me. So I told Miss Shaw I didn't want to skip ahead because then I wouldn't see my friends from my own grade at recess. I kept saying how it was already bad enough being stuck in the smart kids' class all day, but Miss Shaw butted in and said they don't divide up the classes by intelligence. Which is baloney, because my homeroom is full of dorky kids with glasses.

But lately I haven't been having fun with my normal friends either. All they talk about are clothes and boys, and Leslie and Lana started planning what they'll wear to school an entire week in advance. They even dress as twins sometimes, which makes me want to puke. So just because I care more about reading books than trading Sasson jeans or entering the *Teen Beat* modeling contest, now even my friends think I'm unique. Except I have no trouble telling *them* that maybe they're just incredibly boring. Obviously, I'm not too popular anymore.

If you ask me, it was a lot easier being a little kid because I just said what I wanted all the time without thinking about it first. But now Mom and Dad are always explaining how it's not polite to say certain things. So even if someone really *is* incredibly boring, you're not supposed to actually *tell* them about it. I told Mom and Dad I thought that was a pretty phony rule, but then they said I was being rude, and this was exactly the kind of thing they were talking about in the first place.

I guess as you get older you just have to keep your real feelings inside, like a secret, but I'm kind of a blabbermouth, which gets me in trouble. Especially with Mom. She hates me being unique, so she's always asking questions like: "Why don't you wear your hair down instead of putting it in a ponytail?" "Wouldn't you rather wear cute little sandals instead of those dirty sneakers once in a while?" Yesterday she asked, "Why can't you put on a nice cotton skirt with those cute little sandals for school?" I told her that I *obviously* can't wear cute little sandals and a nice cotton skirt when I'm playing softball in the muddy grass at recess. *Duh.*

But Mom didn't like my "sarcastic tone." If I said this last year, it wouldn't have been such a big deal. But because of this new rule about keeping your feelings a secret, I'm not allowed to watch TV this week. That's my usual punishment for saying how I really feel. Especially if it's in a sarcastic tone.

The same thing happened when Alan Strauss came over today. He's my friend Erica's dad, and Erica's parents are both friends with my parents. Erica's mom, Sheila, calls Alan "The Devil" because he left her three years ago for this young secretary named Candy from his office. I thought it was funny that Candy's parents named her after a food, but Erica's mom said it's a perfect name for her because The Devil probably eats her all the time. I figured Sheila meant that Alan takes Candy out to dinner a lot, but Mom said Sheila's been acting pretty crazy since The Devil left her. Mom feels bad for Sheila, and that's why my parents haven't had Alan over since the divorce.

I didn't want to see Alan either, so after I said hi to him I went upstairs. That's when I heard Alan tell my parents that he didn't recognize me at first because I look so different from the last time he saw me. I mean, it's true I still had blondish hair back then, but I don't think I look *that* different. Alan said I really changed a lot, though. Then I heard Mom explain how I'm at this awkward stage girls go through. Except I could hardly hear her because she whispered the words "awkward stage" the way she whispers "nose job" when she tells her friends things like, "It's not the henna that makes Judy look younger, it's her *nose job*."

But Alan didn't whisper like Mom, so I heard exactly what he said next. His voice got really sad, like he was giving one of those speeches at someone's funeral where you talk about all the great things you remember about the person, even if you couldn't stand them when they were alive. "Lori was such a gorgeous child," he said. "She was always the prettiest . . ." but then his voice kind of drifted off, like he might start crying any second. DEAD AT ELEVEN, because I used to be so gorgeous. I wanted to tell Alan that his young secretary, Candy, probably went through an awkward stage once, too—and not that long ago either—but then I remembered the rule about how you can't say what you feel anymore.

That's why I went back downstairs where Alan was having cocktails with Mom and Dad. I walked right up to Alan and said that if he couldn't say something nice about me, he shouldn't say anything at all. Then I told him that even if he thinks I'm not gorgeous anymore, it's rude to say everything you're feeling. I figured Mom and Dad would be proud of me for showing Alan the new rule they've been trying to teach me, but instead Dad's face turned red and Mom kind of gasped. The worst part was, I had to apologize to Alan even though everyone knew I wasn't sorry. So I guess the new rule is more than just Don't Say What You Really Feel. It's also Say What You Really *Don't* Feel.

After Alan left, Mom and Dad told me I was being a smart aleck. "I'm surprised at you, Lori Ellen," Mom said. Mom and Dad always use my middle name when they're mad at me, like I'm from Texas and have a sister named Laura Lee. "You're go- ing to have to watch your mouth from now on," Dad said. I tried explaining that I can't *see* my mouth unless I'm looking in a mirror, but that just made Dad shake his head at me, which I guess meant that I'm hopeless but it would be rude to say so. He just kept shaking his head like every other adult and asked, "Who do you think you are, young lady?"

Dad didn't wait for an answer, because then he left with Mom so I could "think about things." I was supposed to think about how rude I was to Alan. But I guess I was thinking more about Dad's question, "Who do you think you are, young lady?" Because if I was allowed to say what I feel, I'd probably say, "I have no idea anymore."

# Captain of Justice

In school today, Mrs. Rivers gave me a B– on the essay I wrote about my family. She said it was because I went off the subject, but I didn't really go off the subject. I just *added* to the subject, which should have gotten me a *higher* grade since I did extra work.

But when I complained to Mrs. Rivers about it, she told me I should have done the exact assignment. "Every assignment has become an armed battle with you," she said, like we were in the middle of World War Three over an essay. Obviously, Mrs. Rivers exaggerates a lot. But she was probably talking about last week's assignment, the one on our favorite hobby. Mine was on chess, except I did the essay in the shape of a chessboard where each piece I drew was code for one letter of the alphabet. All you had to do was crack the code, then you could read the essay.

"Please see me immediately," was the only thing written on my hobby paper when I got it back. I thought maybe Mrs. Rivers was planning on asking me to ditto it off for the class since teachers ask me to ditto off my assignments a lot. But when I went to see her at the end of class, she grabbed the paper from my hand and asked, "What *is* this?!" "It's my hobby essay," I said, even though I already wrote "Hobby Essay" in big purple letters on the top of the page. I asked Mrs. Rivers if she wanted me to go get those giant glasses she wears off her desk so she could see my essay better, but that's when she started shaking her head at me. It always scares me when Mrs. Rivers does that because she wears a wig and I keep thinking it might come flying off her head.

"Don't be smart with me, dear," she said. Mrs. Rivers is also pretty old and she's always calling her students "dear," like all twenty of us are her grandchildren. I wasn't trying to be smart, but when Mrs. Rivers kept shaking her head at me I figured she probably never cracked the code on my essay, even though I drew a key on the bottom corner that showed which chess piece went with which letter of the alphabet. So I started showing Mrs. Rivers how to read the essay using the key, but I guess she didn't feel like doing that. She just told me that this is her classroom, not Bobby Fischer's, and in her classroom students write in words, not chess pieces.

Anyway, today Mrs. Rivers said that for the family essay, I was supposed to write a single Power Paragraph. I told Mrs. Rivers that I did write a single Power Paragraph, it's just that I also wrote lots of other paragraphs after that, so I should have gotten an A. Then we got into a big argument about it. Finally Mrs. Rivers admitted it was probably unfair to mark me off for doing more than the assignment asked for, but she still wouldn't change my grade. "You're just going to have to learn that life isn't fair, dear," she said. Then she closed the grade book.

I was still mad at Mrs. Rivers when I got to PE. I finished first in running laps, so I was sitting on the playground drawing chalk chess pieces on the bottom of my sneakers and thinking about life being unfair. That's when Miss Drabin came over and said she picked four girls to go to the boys' PE class each Friday, and I was one of them. She said we would be more "challenged" in the boys' class, but you can't believe Miss Drabin about being challenged. Miss Drabin's so prissy that if you tell her you have cramps, you'll get to skip PE for a whole week, even if you haven't gotten your period yet. Besides, you can't play real sports if you're wearing short tennis skirts and Keds with fluffy pom-poms on the laces. That's what Miss Drabin wears for PE.

The boys' class was playing softball when we got there, and no one wanted us on their team because they thought we would be bad players—being girls and all. So when I got up to the plate, all the boys moved in really close, like I could only hit the ball about an inch. I thought their teacher, Mr. Brodsky, would make them stop being such morons, but he was too busy staring at Miss Drabin bending over in her short tennis skirt on the other side of the playground. So since Mr. Brodsky obviously wasn't helping, I came up with a plan of my own. On the first pitch, I ducked out of the way to make everyone think I was scared of the ball. I even made my eyes tear a little on purpose. Mom can make her eyes tear like that, especially if she wants Dad to buy her something really expensive. It worked, too, because then the whole group of boys moved even closer to the plate until no one was left in the outfield.

That's when I heard all the boys laughing about girls belonging in the girls' PE class. Some of them were even sticking their butts out and talking in high voices, saying things like, "Oooo, I'm just a girl, I'm soooo scared"—especially Scott, the pitcher. The rest of the boys were still laughing because Scott kept saying I held the bat like a girl. Whatever *that* means. So I pretended that Scott's round face was the ball he was holding. Then all of a sudden the second pitch came, and I whacked the ball over everyone's head and hit a home run. I couldn't believe it! I mean, I knew I could hit the ball into the outfield, but I was pretty surprised when it went flying over the fence. I guess I was really mad at Scott. "Maybe next time *you* should hold the bat like a girl," I said when I got back to home plate, but Scott acted like he didn't hear me. Nasty people hate it when you're nasty back to them.

At the end of the period, we had to pick teams for next week. Both team leaders wanted me on their team because of the home run, and they even got in a fistfight about it. It was pretty exciting. But when Mr. Brodsky finally noticed what was going on and told the boys to stop fighting, they didn't listen, and now they have to sit the next game out. You should have seen their faces after Mr. Brodsky made *me* one of the new team captains. I figured he did it to kiss up to Miss Drabin, but I didn't care.

After school, I told Mom about how both boys wanted me on their team, and she got excited, too. "The boys are fighting over you already," she said, like I was talking about a school dance. I don't think she heard the part about the home run. So I never told Mom about being made team captain, because she probably would have thought I was made middle school prom queen or something. But it's okay I guess, because those boys got what they deserved.

And besides, I think Mrs. Rivers was wrong about what she said today. Sometimes life is fair.

# Power Paragraph

Maybe I really *am* as different as everyone says, because ever since Mrs. Rivers gave me that B– on my family essay, I can't say "be." I can *write* it, but I'm too scared to say it. I keep thinking if I say "be," I'll get a B on my next paper or quiz or even my report card. I'd rather *die* than get a B on my report card! But if you really want to know what happened with the essay, this is what the assignment sheet said:

FAMILY BIOGRAPHY ASSIGNMENT

For Friday, write one POWER PARAGRAPH—a topic sentence with at least three main supporting idea sentences—in which you describe the members of your family. You may, FOR EXTRA CREDIT, include supporting sentences for your main supporting ideas. No late papers will be accepted.

Anyway, here's what I wrote:

My family consists of my mother, my father, my brother, and my bird, Chrissy. (That was my topic sentence.) My mother is very pretty, but she doesn't like to think too much. (Supporting idea #1.) She always has her eyes slanted and her mouth open, like in those model pictures in Mom's magazines that are supposed to be so sexy, but I think my mother keeps her mouth that way so she'll always be ready to scream at me for doing something wrong. (Supporting sentence for supporting idea #1. It's kind of a run-on sentence, but it was supposed to be for extra credit anyway.) My father isn't very handsome, but he likes to think all the time. (Supporting idea #2.) If you ever ask Dad about feelings, he'll change the subject to something you can think about logically. (Supporting sentence for supporting idea #2.) My fourteen-year-old brother, David, used to be my best friend, but lately he turns on his stereo and closes his door without letting me in. (Supporting idea #3.) I don't think he likes me anymore. (Supporting sentence for supporting idea #3.) I also have a parakeet named after Chrissy from the TV show *Three's Company,* and David has a parakeet named Jack. (Supporting idea #4.) I named her Chrissy instead of Janet because Mom said that a bird with a yellow head would match the wallpaper in my bedroom better, and Chrissy has blond hair on the show. (Supporting sentence for supporting idea #4.) Even though she's just a bird, Chrissy's my best friend now. (Second supporting sentence for supporting idea #4.) That's because she's the only normal member of my family. (Supporting sentence for second supporting sentence for supporting idea #4.)

That was the part where I followed the exact assignment. But Mrs. Rivers said I'd only get an A if I rewrote the rest of the essay using the "proper transitions," and I really wanted the A. So to make her happy, I threw in all the Power Paragraph Transition Words from our list:

| although | in conclusion | otherwise |
| as a result | in contrast | perhaps |
| as discussed | in other words | previously |
| evidently | in sum | specifically |
| for example | likewise | therefore |
| furthermore | moreover | to begin with |
| however | nevertheless | yet |
| in addition | on the other hand | |

Here's what I wrote after the part about Chrissy being my best friend:

In conclusion, those are the members of my family. However, if you really want to know about someone, you have to start at the very beginning. Specifically, you can't just walk in when they're adults and understand where they came from. Otherwise, it's like being late for a movie. For example, you never understand what's going on in a movie unless you've seen the very beginning, when the movie stars meet each other, or some big crime happens that the movie stars spend the entire movie trying to solve. Therefore, you really have to get to movies on time, even if there's a lot of traffic and nowhere to park.

To begin with, my mom's beginning was in Salt Lake City, Utah. I wasn't around then, obviously, but I've heard about her life from other relatives. Specifically, they said that where Mom grew up, most people were Mormons, but Mom's family was Jewish. In addition, when Mom was just seven years old, her father, who owned a jewelry store, suddenly dropped dead from a heart attack right in the middle of the store. Specifically, it was around lunchtime. More specifically, he was only in his forties, which is old, but it's a young age to die at. Personally, I feel bad for Mom because she really loved visiting her dad at his store. Evidently, the reason Mom gets such a big kick out of diamond rings is that they remind her of her dad's jewelry store. In sum, that is all I really know about Mom before I was born.

However, I usually think about Mom as that seven-year-old girl, because in a lot of ways, Mom still acts like a kid. For example, she's always crying over dumb things. As a result, she always carries around several bunches of tissues in her big purse, and when her eyes start to tear up, out come those tissues, just like clockwork. Specifically, Mom usually cries when she's saying good-bye to people, but she can also tear up on purpose, which is why I think she should have been an actress. More specifically, she'd be great on one of those sappy soap operas she loves to watch. In sum, she's a very dramatic person.

Moreover, just like a soap opera star, Mom expects people to wait on her. For example, she doesn't like to remember things that other adults have to remember. Like remembering where you're parked in the mall, or remembering where you put your house keys, or knowing where your purse is when your kid needs lunch money and is late for school. For example, every time Mom is ready to leave the house, she calls out for our housekeeper, Maria, even if she doesn't need Maria at all. Then Maria always has to tell her that her sunglasses are on her head, her keys are in her hand, and her daughter has been waiting in the car for the past ten minutes. On the other hand, most adults can probably remember these things without a housekeeper.

Nevertheless, even though Mom acts like a kid, she loves dressing up like a beautiful woman. For example, she doesn't have many interests in addition to shopping. In contrast, whenever I go to friends' houses after school, we do puzzles, paint, bake things, and play Scrabble with their moms. On the other hand, the only thing I ever do with my mom is go shopping. Which is never fun, because Mom spends hours dressing me up to go shopping, even though the whole point of shopping is to buy *better* clothes than the ones you already have. Yet, that is just my opinion.

Finally, the only other thing that Mom likes to do is go to the movies. Specifically, she loves sappy, romantic movies so she can tear up and use all those tissues she keeps in her big purse. However, Mom and I usually don't like the same movies. For example, she didn't like my favorite movie, *Star Wars,* probably because no one goes shopping in that movie. More specifically, all Mom said after the movie ended was how pretty Princess Leia was. In sum, she totally missed the point.

In contrast, although my mom cries and screams, my dad is mostly silent. To begin with, my father is from Washington, D.C., and his family moved to Beverly Hills when he was in high school. Likewise, Dad's parents were also silent, and they died when I was about four years old. Therefore, I don't know much about his beginning. However, I do know that my father is very smart, very tense, and likes to spend a lot of time alone in his study, especially when Mom is crying, screaming, or meeting with the decorator. On the other hand, Dad has many interests, such as chess, photography, politics, art history, and taking apart mechanical things.

Furthermore, Dad is a stockbroker, which means that all day long he watches the numbers on the New York Stock Exchange and tries to outsmart the Dow Jones industrial average by picking stocks he thinks are better. For example, if you want to buy a stock, Dad will try to figure out if its price-to-earnings ratio makes it good enough to buy before all the other stockbrokers figure out the same thing. In other words, you have to buy low and sell high. Personally, I think the reason Dad is so great at his job is because he's the most logical stockbroker around.

Nevertheless, Dad bugs me sometimes, but not like Mom does. For example, Dad's nicer than Mom, but he likes to pretend that he doesn't hear Mom screaming at me. Specifically, he never says anything when Mom's telling me how abnormal I am for a girl, or how I care too much about math, or how much she wishes I wasn't so unique. More specifically, he never says, "You're wrong about Lori. She's really very interesting and funny and smart and pretty, so leave her alone." Therefore, I'm always worried about what Mom might say, and what Dad might not. In sum, that is all I know about my dad.

In conclusion, I have nothing to add about my brother, David, or my bird, Chrissy. That is because I don't play with David much anymore and, as discussed previously, Chrissy is too normal to write about. THE END.

I really ruined the essay with all those "specifically" and "in sum" words I had to add, but as long as I get an A, I don't care. By the way, you know how I said I'll die if I say "be"? Well, don't worry about me dying, because I have a way of taking it back if I say it by mistake. All I do is repeat the exact sentence I said with "be" in it, but I say "A" where the "be" was. Then I'm safe until the next "be" comes up, and when it does, I just say "A" all over again. Except I usually whisper it so people don't think I'm a complete weirdo, even though Leslie and Lana always cross their fingers and count to thirteen when they pass a cemetery, and no one ever calls *them* weirdos.

# Real Women Don't Eat Dessert

I guess you should also know about my sidewalk thing.

The truth is, I don't even know *why* I started it. I just remember *when* it started because it was the Wednesday before Thanksgiving. I usually walk to and from school with Julie since we live on the same block, but Julie and her family went to New York for Thanksgiving, so I had to walk home by myself. I was wearing shorts because it was warm and sunny out, like it always is in California, and I was thinking about how lucky Julie was since she'd get to see snow. But then I couldn't stop thinking about how we don't have snow in California, and how the trees don't turn pretty colors, and how we don't have neat old houses with attics and basements, and how we wear the same clothes all year round, and how everyone looks exactly the same here. The more I thought about it, the more I noticed that *nothing* changes in California.

Then I was thinking about how we hardly even get *rain* in California, and what a *boring* state it is compared to all the others, and that's when I saw this lady walking toward me on the sidewalk up ahead. She was humming a song, and you could tell she was pretty happy. I mean, I couldn't understand how she could be so happy and live in California at the same time. Unless she was just visiting for the holidays, but I doubted it.

Anyway, we were on this really narrow sidewalk, the kind where one of us would have to walk on the grass when we passed each other, but since the lady was wearing high heels and I was only wearing sneakers, it would have been easier for me to go around. But then I decided that there was no way I would ruin my walk for someone who didn't even *care* how boring California is. So when we got close enough so one of us would have to move, I looked the lady right in the eye and kept on walking. We practically crashed into each other, but at the last second, the lady stepped onto the grass and let me by. Except she kind of sighed when she did it, and she stopped humming, too. Then I felt bad about what I did, but at least I didn't have to move out of the way if I didn't want to. Believe me, I always have to do things I don't want to.

But here's the worst part: Ever since that day, I've been doing the sidewalk thing even when Julie *is* there. Plus I make sure not to step on any lines. Luckily, Julie hasn't noticed because we don't walk home together much anymore, and in the morning on the way to school she's always half asleep. Julie sleeps in so late most days that she never has time for any breakfast, so her mom always packs her half a bagel smothered in diet cream cheese to eat on the way. Which is kind of funny, if you knew Julie's mom.


Julie's mom is always on some new diet, but if you want my opinion, she never looks like she's losing any weight. I know all about her diets because Julie bores me to death talking about them. This morning, when I was trying not to step on any lines on the sidewalk, Julie told me about her mom's latest diet. All of Julie's mom's diets have phony names like "The No-Temptation Diet" or "The Effortless Diet" or "Thin in Three Days."

This one's called "The Authentic Movie Star Diet," I guess so people will think that everyone who's a movie star has been following this diet for years. Which is baloney, because most movie stars eat at fancy restaurants all the time.

I could tell you in one sentence what The Authentic Movie Star Diet is, but someone else wrote an entire book about it. Basically, all you do is eat one kind of food each week, but you can eat as much of it as you want. This week, Julie's mom is eating only bananas, but she can eat millions of them if she wants. Next week, she'll eat only meats, then the week after she'll eat only breads. I don't know what comes next, but I still don't think you need to write a whole book about it.

Once when I was over at Julie's house, I read some of her mom's diet books just to see why you need so many books to tell you how to eat. They all said different things, though. Like one said to eat lots of carbohydrates for energy, and another said don't ever eat carbohydrates because they're fattening. They never even told you what a carbohydrate *was*. One book said a carbohydrate was a piece of bread, but another book said it was a bowl of pasta. They made no sense, which is probably why Julie's mom never loses any weight.

So on the way to school today, Julie told me that she might go on The Authentic Movie Star Diet, too. I told Julie that I didn't think she was fat, but Julie said her mom wants her to lose some weight so she won't be chubby and sad as a teenager. She even sent her to a nutritionist to plan her meals, but Julie's always starving on that plan. I have to admit, I kind of peeked at Julie's body today just to see if maybe she really was fat and I never noticed—but I still don't think she's fat. It's true she wears a bigger jean size than some girls at school, but that's just because she's much taller than us, too. She grew like six inches last year.

That's probably why Julie steals muffins from the cafeteria sometimes. The first time I saw Julie steal a muffin I thought about telling on her, but first of all, I'm not a tattletale, and second of all, it's not *Julie's* fault, if you really think about it. So then I almost called this hot line for abused kids because I thought it was sad that Julie's mom was starving her. I saw a commercial on TV that said you can call this hot line and they won't ever tell the abusers who reported them. Julie's mom can scream pretty loud, which is why I wouldn't want her to know if I reported her. I'd probably have a heart attack if she came over to my house and screamed at me after school.

But I never ended up calling the hot line anyway. That's because I started noticing that Julie's mom wasn't that different from everyone else's mom, and I didn't want to report the whole *city*. I mean, everyone's mom loves talking about their diets and how full you can get from eating lots of salads. They're always eating lots of salads before weddings and fancy occasions so they can fit into sexy dresses. I'd just buy a bigger dress that fits right instead of starving myself for five days in a row, but all my friends' moms would rather starve themselves.

This year, though, Julie's mom started making us girls starve ourselves, too, even though we don't have any sexy dresses to fit into. Every time I eat dinner over at Julie's, her mom says, "Now girls, remember to leave the table wanting a little something more." Which makes no sense, because the whole *point* of eating is to make you full again.

Then my mom started doing it, too. Right when I was about to call the hot line, I was in the kitchen baking Toll House cookies after school and when I reached for a second cookie, Mom told me to save the cookies for "the guys." She meant Dad and David. I asked Mom why I should save the cookies for the guys, since *I* baked them and they wouldn't even taste good later when they got cold. But Mom didn't give me a reason. She just kept saying that you should always save desserts for the guys, kind of like the way she says that you should always put your napkin on your lap or say thank you when someone says how adorable your outfit is. I wanted to tell her how stupid this rule was, but then I'd be breaking those other rules I have to follow now that I'm older, like Don't Say What You Really Feel, and Don't Use a Sarcastic Tone.

So I didn't say anything, but then I started noticing that whenever Mom bought stuff at the bakery, she'd never eat any of it. And if I ever wanted to eat a pastry or some cookies, she'd keep telling me to save them for the guys. I guess I could pretty much understand saving desserts for Dad, since he's an adult and you're supposed to respect your parents and stuff, but I didn't think there was any rule about respecting your *brother*. So finally I asked again why I have to save desserts for David when he never has to save desserts for me.

This time Mom gave me a reason. "David's a growing boy and he needs his energy," she said. Then I asked Mom why I didn't need to eat the same food since I'm a growing girl. I mean, I'm not gonna be 4'8" for the rest of my life. And besides, Dad stopped growing a long time ago. "It's just different," was all she said. Mom's pretty bad at explaining things, so she always leaves the "why" questions for Dad to answer, and if Dad's not around, she tells me to stop asking why all the time. So I didn't ask why when I went downstairs at night and found Mom standing over the kitchen sink stuffing a chocolate chip cookie into her mouth. To tell you the truth, I haven't asked why since.

But the other thing I noticed is that whenever we're in a restaurant and Mom can't finish her food, she offers it to David and Dad, but never to me. Except she doesn't say, "Do you want some of my chicken?" She just points one of her long fingernails at her plate, makes a really grossed-out face, then says, "I need help with this." The funny thing is, Mom never even waits to hear if David or Dad *wants* more food. She just dumps it on their plates while she's telling them how full she is. Which obviously can't be true, because if she was so full she wouldn't sneak down to the kitchen late at night to stuff cookies into her mouth.

# Thunder Thighs

I swear, Valentine's Day makes me want to puke. It's such a phony holiday. Our homeroom teacher, Mr. Miller, made a rule that we had to give a valentine card to every single kid in the class, including the ones we can't stand. So today everyone got the same exact valentine cards, even though we all know that Chris Caplan would *never* give a card to that chubby Evelyn girl who picks her nose and puts boogers under the rim of her desk. Every other day he calls her the Booger Girl, but today he wrote her a card that said, "Happy Valentine's Day."

The reason I'm talking about Chris is that Samantha invited him to this big Valentine's Day party she was having after school. I've been to Samantha's parties before, but it was my first time going to what Mom kept calling a "boy-girl" party. Mom said this was different from a regular party because at this party we'd be playing games like spin the bottle. So I asked how she knew what we'd be doing, and she admitted that she saw the invitation on my desk. I'm telling you, nothing's private anymore.

The invitation Mom saw looked like a newspaper ad, but instead of saying, SALES LADY WANTED, it said, GUESTS WANTED FOR A PARTY. Then when you opened up the invitation, it said,

NO EXPERIENCE NECESSARY. Ha. Ha. The person who made this
card probably thought he was hilarious, but not as hilarious as
Samantha thinks *she* is. On the inside of my invitation, Samantha took a bright red marker and underlined the part about no
experience being necessary. Then she drew about a hundred exclamation marks. Real funny.

Samantha did this because a month ago, Tracy Karp had a
"boy-girl" party—the first one anyone in our grade ever had—but
I wasn't invited. Partly because I'm not too popular anymore, but
mostly because Tracy hates me for not letting her copy my homework. I told Tracy that if she really wanted to be friends with me
she wouldn't care if I didn't let her copy my homework, but Tracy
said if I was a true friend, I'd let her copy it. Then I told Tracy
that if I was stupid enough to believe that, my homework
wouldn't be *worth* copying in the first place. But Tracy dumped
me anyway. Of course, I still got a valentine card from her today
because of Mr. Miller's phony rule.

Anyway, after Tracy's party last month, everyone who went
acted like they knew all about kissing. I sort of knew they were
lying about what happened, but every time I looked at the invitation, I got scared that the people who went to Tracy's party
would look sexy at Samantha's party and I wouldn't. Not that
I'm positive about what sexy means, exactly. I usually just think
about being pretty—like having a pretty face or pretty hair or a
pretty smile or something—but lately I've been wondering if I
look sexy instead of pretty. Or sexy and pretty *at the same time.* If
that's even possible.

Like a few days ago, we had this heat wave and David had
some friends over swimming. I was practicing my run off the
diving board when I heard David's friend Philip say that I have
"a body." Which is a pretty weird thing to say, because I've *always* had a body. But then I figured that maybe you don't exist
until you have a certain kind of body, or a sexy body, or something. So I asked David if he thought I had a sexy body, and he
said I was perfect the way I was, and that I should stop worry-

ing about it now because I'll have to worry about it all the time when I'm a teenager.

But I still couldn't stop thinking about what Philip said about me having a body. It was really bugging me, so before I went to bed that night, I stood in front of the full-length mirror and kept trying to figure out what made me have a body all of a sudden. I must have been there for hours. But no matter how much I looked, I still didn't feel sexy. The truth is, I don't even fit all the way into a training bra yet, unlike Leslie and Lana, who love wearing twin baseball shirts with magenta sleeves and ITTY BITTY TITTY COMMITTEE in glitter across the front, just so everyone will look.

Anyway, I kept trying to figure out what makes a person sexy, and then I thought about those people in *A Chorus Line.* You could tell *they* were sexy. Last summer, I went with my grandma to see *A Chorus Line,* which was this musical about all these beautiful actresses who wanted to be in a big show. There was a song in the show called "Tits and Ass," and even though my grandma kept coughing every time the actress sang the words "tits" or "ass," it made me think maybe that's what makes a person sexy—her tits and her ass. The actress who sang the song had pretty big boobs, and I guess her butt was okay.

So when I was looking in the mirror, I started wondering if maybe I'd look sexy if my boobs looked like that actress's. Then I went into my closet to find something to stuff into my T-shirt. I wanted to stuff in two baseballs, but I'm really more of a softball player, and those balls were *way* too big. I only had one baseball, though, so I stuffed in one baseball and one softball, which made me look more retarded than sexy. I also looked retarded with the two huge softballs stuffed under my T-shirt because the rest of my body is pretty skinny. Which is weird, because my Barbie doll never looked that way with her huge boobs

and skinny body. So finally I thought about stuffing a bunch of
tissues into my T-shirt instead, but everyone's always talking
about how there's a paper shortage and I didn't want to waste
the trees. I probably would have needed a whole box of tissues
to look like Barbie.

But I really wanted to look sexy for Samantha's party, so before school today, I tried on about a hundred different outfits
and ended up wearing my blue culottes, my rainbow T-shirt
that's tight around my boobs, and my gold chain. I thought I
looked okay in that outfit, but at breakfast I was reading the
chess column and next to it was a picture of a model in a white
lacy blouse with these long, flowing sleeves. The lady in the picture was wearing tight jeans with the blouse, and I'm not sure
what it was about her exactly, but I could tell *she* looked sexy. So
after breakfast, I ran upstairs and put on my own white lacy
blouse, my tight black jeans, and my new Korkease sandals. I
still didn't feel sexy, but I couldn't change clothes again because
I had to get to homeroom and Mr. Miller always calls roll the
second the bell rings. Believe me, he loves giving people tardies.

Samantha's party wasn't until 4:00, and by that time I finally got excited about going and seeing Chris there. He's my
type. Mom's always talking about how hunky all these movie
stars are, like Robert Redford or Burt Reynolds, but to me they
just look like someone's dad with longer hair and a suntan.
Chris doesn't look anything like Robert Redford, but I still
think he's cute, and he also knows how to play chess. Plus he
has a crush on me. I found out about Chris liking me when
Leslie heard Chris whispering to his best friend, Michael, in
history. Leslie said Chris told Michael that he liked me, but
when I asked Leslie what his exact words were, she said she
didn't remember. I think Leslie likes Chris, too.

But I knew it was true, because a couple of days later, a bunch
of us were on the playground after school working on a dance
routine that we're doing to the music from *Welcome Back, Kotter.*
Tracy's mom was teaching us this really slow, sexy dance for the

talent show. Some of the boys who were outside playing ball came over to watch us, and they were making fun of us and telling us how spazzy we looked, but Tracy's mom explained how that's just their way of flirting. Which makes no sense, because if you like someone that way, you shouldn't make fun of them. I mean, Robert Redford would never call Barbra Streisand a spaz just to let her know he *likes* her. Anyway, we were all swinging our hips on the playground, and after a while I even forgot the boys were there. I think it was the first time I ever felt sexy, but now I can't remember what it felt like. It only lasted about a second or so. But everyone said Chris was staring at me the whole time, so I couldn't wait to see him at Samantha's party.

The trouble with Samantha's party was partly that all the people from Tracy's boy-girl party were there, partly that everyone was wearing the same lacy blouse and Korkease as me, and mostly that Mom was right about playing spin the bottle. So when Chris spun the bottle and it pointed right at me, everyone who went to Tracy's party started laughing and making cracks about how madly in love I was with Chris—even though Chris was also being nasty, which I guess could have meant he was *flirting* with me. But I wouldn't say that what we did was kiss. The rules of the game were that we had to touch lips for sixty seconds, and that's all we did. I mean, you can't get too romantic with a bunch of popular kids sitting around you in a circle and counting off to sixty at the top of their lungs.

Then it was my turn to spin the bottle. I swear I didn't mean to do this, but when I spun the bottle it accidentally landed in front of Chris, which made everyone yell "Oooooo" all at once. That meant I had to stand in a closet with Chris for five minutes, except we didn't go into an actual closet. Instead we went into the TV room. Samantha's dad works at ABC, so her family has a whole room with just a big-screen TV and a Betamax machine. On the way in, Chris grabbed some potato chips and stuffed them in his mouth, which I thought was kind of a stupid thing to do if he was planning on kissing me. They were the onion-flavored kind. Robert Redford wouldn't do that either.

It didn't matter, though, because it turned out that Chris was more interested in the big TV than he was in me. For the whole five minutes, we sat miles away from each other on this huge, mushy sofa. No one even said a word, except for the time when Chris asked me if I wanted a potato chip. I had nothing else to do and we obviously weren't about to kiss, so I took one. I spent the rest of the time worrying about what might happen if I got stuck in the sofa and couldn't get up by myself. Then someone came to get us and we went back into the living room where everyone made kissing sounds at us, even though we never kissed in the first place. Some boy-girl party.

I thought I might die if we had to keep playing, but then all of a sudden the boys went into the TV room and the girls ran to the bathroom so they could flip their hair a million times in front of the mirror. I hate flipping my hair, so I just waited out in the hallway. That's when I heard the boys talking about us. They were teasing Michael because he has a huge crush on Tracy, and I guess he didn't want to admit it. So when everyone started saying things like, "Oh, Tracy, I love you sooooo much," Michael tried acting like he didn't care about her at all. "Yeah, right. She's got thunder thighs," he said, even though Tracy doesn't. She's just not extra skinny like Leslie and Lana. But no one teased Michael after he said that. I guess it's pretty obvious that no one could ever like a girl who has thunder thighs.

I kind of wanted to hear what Chris would say about me, but then all the girls came out of the bathroom. That's when everyone started throwing potato chips at each other, but I was just thinking about the TV show *Happy Days*. There was this one show where Richie was going out with a really smart girl, and Fonzie asked him, "Do you have a hot date with Miss IQ?" Fonzie was being sarcastic because he figured the smart girl would be a total nerd. But the girl they called Miss IQ was really pretty, even though they made her wear those ugly black horn-rimmed glasses on the date so she'd look intelligent. Like you can't be pretty and smart at the same time. I was thinking about that show because if the boys in the TV room started talking about me, I'd want them to ask Chris, "What was it like kissing Miss IQ?" I mean, I'd much rather be called Miss IQ than Thunder Thighs, even if it's meant as an insult. Nothing could be worse than being called Thunder Thighs.

When I finally got home from the party, Mom and Dad asked me if I had a good time. "It was okay," I said, which was a lie, but if you give my parents more than a yes or no answer, they always asks thousands of nosy questions. So I started going upstairs, but I guess Mom could tell I wasn't exactly thrilled. That's why she told me to march back downstairs so she could give me some advice on how to have more fun at boy-girl parties.

Mom's advice was that if I wanted to have more fun at the next party, maybe I should wear lip gloss for a little shine, like the other girls do. Then she went on about how a woman needs to wear makeup if she wants to attract a man, and how even if she's just going to the corner drugstore, a woman should always have some lipstick on because you never know who you might run into. Mom has about twenty different lipsticks and she's always running into people she knows when she's shopping.

I told Mom that I wasn't planning on wearing makeup, even when I'm older, but then she asked, "How can you walk out of the house without a little lip gloss on?" Like if a lady walked outside without any lip gloss, a huge lightning bolt would suddenly crash down from the sky and kill her. "You just open the door and walk outside," I answered, but then Dad told me not to talk to Mom that way, and Mom told me that my tone wasn't very ladylike.

Now that I think about it, I don't know what makes me puke more: Valentine's Day or being ladylike.

# Sex Education

Today in school we finally learned about sex. I was excited because I waited the whole year to learn about it from someone besides Mom and Dad. That's because when I asked them, "If sex happens in the vagina, what are the boobs for?" Dad said, "How about a game of chess after dinner?" and the next day Mom took me to the library to check out some books because she hates when I ask questions. The books were pretty stupid, though. One was called *What's Happening to Me?* and inside there were lots of colored drawings of boys and girls with different-sized patches of pubic hair. The pubic hair patches kept getting bigger on every page until the boys and girls finally turned into men and women on the last one. Like the ending was supposed to be a big surprise.

In another book, though, there was a lady who had blond hair on her head, but black hair on her vagina, so I wondered if maybe dyeing your vagina hair black was supposed to be sexy. But when I asked Mom about it, she giggled and looked at her pumps, then she turned to Dad and said, "Did you hear what Lori just asked?" I figured that meant "no" about the black vagina hair being sexy, but then David answered my question.

He told me that the lady in the drawing dyes her *head* hair blond, not her other hair black. Then he called me a moron for the rest of the day, but I didn't care. I was pretty surprised that he knew anything about sex. I mean, we have the same parents.

After that, I was pretty curious about sex. But when I finally learned about it today, it wasn't that exciting. I guess not knowing about it made me think it would be this *supernatural* thing with shooting stars and fireworks and stuff. But the best part of sex education turned out to be the childbirth part. If you want my opinion, *that* was supernatural.

In the film we saw in school, a woman was giving birth to a baby girl. Her husband was there holding her hand the whole time, and the woman was smiling and all the doctors kept telling her how great she was doing, even though she was breathing really hard and sweating like a pig. It didn't look that fun. But then the supernatural part finally came. All of a sudden, the baby's head popped out! That's when the baby was delivered and they found out it was a girl. The doctor in the movie handed the baby to the mother, and even though I'm not too into sappy stuff, I almost cried when the music came on and they did a close-up of the mother's face. I didn't cry, though, because then our science teacher, Mrs. Jacobs, turned on those overhead fluorescent lights that always give me a headache. It really ruined the mood. Besides, I couldn't wait to go home and tell David about what he's missing by being a boy.

David was at Philip's house when I got home, but Mom was in her closet hanging up some dresses she just bought. I was really excited about this whole childbirth thing, and I wanted to know what it was like when *I* was born. After the movie in school, a girl in my class named Felicity said that every year on her birthday, her mother tells her how the happiest day of her life was the day Felicity was born. Her mom even named her

Felicity because it means "happy" in Spanish. It's true, too, because I asked our housekeeper Maria, and all she speaks is Spanish, practically.

Anyway, when I asked Mom about what it was like the day I was born, I found out it wasn't even close to the happiest day of her life. Which I guess is why I was named Lori instead of Felicity. First of all, Dad wasn't in the delivery room holding Mom's hand, probably because he was in the waiting area pacing around with his *Wall Street Journal.* Mom also said she wasn't smiling like the lady in the movie because when the doctors told her to keep pushing, she was too busy screaming for them to give her more drugs. The lady in the movie didn't take any drugs, but Mom said the reason she took drugs was because she didn't want to feel anything coming out. I guess she meant me.

By the time I did come out, Mom said she was so tired from the drugs that she hardly noticed me. But she also said that it's very important for a new mother to be awake when her baby is first handed to her, so she can check to see if the baby's okay. So when the doctors handed my body to Mom for the very first time, she counted my fingers and toes, checked to see that my nose wouldn't need a nose job, and made sure that my ears didn't stick out funny. "Always check that the ears are flat," Mom warned me, like I might have a baby sometime soon or something.

To tell you the truth, I kind of wasn't interested in hearing any more, but since this was the first time Mom bothered answering one of my questions about sex, I figured I should let her keep talking. Mom was saying how she thought it was rude that the doctors didn't wipe the blood off me right away, so she handed my body back to them to be cleaned. That's probably because Mom loves sending things back, mostly at fancy restaurants where she always finds something wrong with her dinner and blames the waiter, even though *he* wasn't the one who cooked it. I'll bet Mom blamed the doctor for all the blood on my body, even though *he* wasn't the one who put it there. Anyway, all Mom remembered after sending me back to the doctors was that she fell asleep. I guess my nose and ears were okay, though, because then I went off to an incubator.

One thing about Mom is that if *she* feels like talking about something, she'll bore you to death talking about it. So even though Mom never used to want to talk about sex, today she wouldn't stop saying how funny it is that I thought childbirth was supposed to be supernatural. I told her that the lady in the movie also thought childbirth was supernatural, but that just made Mom laugh. "That darling woman has no idea what she's in store for," she said. Mom calls everyone darling, even if she's never met them before and they're only some actress in a school movie. I was wondering why Mom does that when she said, "Just wait, she'll see how supernatural having a child is. Believe me, Lori, the pain only *begins* with childbirth."

I think Mom was trying to be funny because she was still kind of laughing. But then Maria came in with the vacuum cleaner, and Mom said something I couldn't hear and left. Which is fine with me, because I'm not even curious about sex anymore anyway. I wish I never asked about it in the first place.

## Chameleon

I'm never talking to Mom and Dad again. I'm serious. Mom
and Dad said that we're going to Washington, D.C., for two
weeks over the spring vacation, which is only one week long.
That means I'll have to miss the whole week of school before
vacation starts. I tried telling them about all the tests and assignments and parties I'll miss if they make me go, and how
it's *illegal* to take me out of school unless I'm sick. But then
Mom gave Dad her famous look that means I'm making her
nervous, which made Dad say, "End of discussion." That
means you're not allowed to say anything, but if you do, Dad
just keeps on saying, "I said, end of discussion. And that's final." His voice gets really deep, too, like he suddenly turned
into Walter Cronkite. So usually I slam my door really loud,
just so my parents hear *something*.

But the other way my parents end conversations is by walking away and leaving you standing there with no one to hear
you. Then you can't even slam your door in their face. That's
what happened yesterday. Except instead of going to my room,
I decided that I'd sit in the middle of the hallway until dinnertime, kind of like those people on the 6:00 news who hold up

signs and sit in the middle of the street blocking traffic until people notice them. I wasn't planning on budging until Mom and Dad listened to why I'll *die* if I miss school. I figured they'd definitely listen just to get me out of the hallway. But after a while no one seemed to notice I was there. I sort of felt like the chameleon we saw on our field trip to the zoo yesterday. I couldn't stop thinking about it.

The reason our science class went to the zoo was because we were working on our animal unit in the textbook, and Mrs. Jacobs wanted us to see the animals in person. Most of the other kids liked the zebras and koala bears best, but I kept staring at a glass cage that looked like it had nothing in it. We were in the reptile area, and it was hard to see inside the cages because the sun kept shining on the glass and practically blinding you. If you looked really hard, though, you could see all these green lizards and salamanders sitting on a piece of wood way in the back. Except in this one cage, none of us could see anything no matter how hard we looked. Then Mrs. Jacobs explained that there were chameleons in that cage, but you couldn't see them because they had to blend in with the rocks so they wouldn't get eaten. She said that if they wanted to survive, they had to be invisible.

So I was thinking about being invisible, but then I remembered something else that happened at the zoo with Robin. Robin's only been at our school since the beginning of the year, but everyone says she's pretty rebellious. I know because I heard one of the teachers, who isn't even her teacher, call her a "bad seed" to another teacher, who also isn't her teacher. I mean, they don't even know Robin, but she has a reputation for being rebellious. It's so unfair. The only reason Robin has this reputation is because she always wears Kiss concert T-shirts and once drew a black star over her eye like Gene Simmons. Anyway, when we were at the zoo, Mrs. Jacobs wouldn't let Robin buy a T-shirt that said, GIRAFFES DO MORE THAN NECKING.

The part of the T-shirt that Mrs. Jacobs didn't like was the picture of two giraffes having sex right under the words. At least that's what Robin said they were doing, and Robin really wanted the T-shirt. She said it was her allowance money and she could do what she wanted with it, which made sense to me. I didn't hear the whole argument because I was on the other side of the gift shop with the everyone else, but we all heard when Robin shouted, "Fuck you, Darlene!" at the top of her lungs. Darlene is Mrs. Jacobs's first name, and no one *ever* calls her that. Robin was suspended, obviously, but I still think she was right about being allowed to buy the giraffe T-shirt. I mean, it was a funny shirt.

When I remembered what Robin did, I didn't want to be invisible anymore. All of a sudden I wanted to scream "Fuck you!" to my parents the way Robin did to Mrs. Jacobs, even if I'd get punished for it. Nothing could be worse than having to go to Washington the week before vacation starts. If my parents didn't walk away in the middle of our conversation, they'd know that Erica's big party is the week before vacation, that *everyone's* going, and that they're ruining my social life. I mean, Mom knows how important a social life is for a woman. That's all she talks about, practically.

But the worst part is, I'll be missing a whole week of tests and homework assignments! I was thinking about how I might even get a B if I missed a whole week of school, because I wouldn't be there to take good notes. I'll die if I get a B! So that's when I yelled "Fuck you!" at the top of my lungs. Mom and Dad sure listened to that.

All of a sudden, Mom came running out of the bedroom and Dad came running out of his study, like when he makes us do those practice fire drills on the first day of every month. But this was different than a fire drill, because instead of meeting at the bottom of the stairs, Dad spanked me a bunch of times. Mom and Dad believe every word in this child-rearing book they have, but if you ask me, it's a very stupid book. It calls hitting your kid "spankings," even if your kid is eleven. I kept screaming for Dad to stop, but Mom just stood there crying because I hurt her feelings when I said the F-word. Then I started crying, too, and Dad finally stopped spanking me, but all of a sudden I yelled "Fuck you!" again. I swear, I didn't mean to, but I liked saying it so much I couldn't help it. That's when Dad told me I was grounded until we go to Washington. Like I have a car and ever go anywhere anyway. Then Mom and Dad left me in the hallway again.

I don't know how long I stayed there, but it must have been a pretty long time because even after everyone went to bed, I was still sitting out there on the floor. I guess I really did blend in like a chameleon, since no one seemed to know I was there. Which is good, because at least they stopped punishing me. So that's why I'm not talking to Mom and Dad anymore. I mean, maybe you really *do* have to be invisible to survive.

# Life, Liberty, and the Pursuit of Happiness

You wouldn't believe how awful it is being trapped here in Washington. If you want my opinion, most parents would do *something* if their kid didn't say a single word for a week straight. But Mom and Dad are acting like it's perfectly normal for me to be quiet, like I was born without a tongue. I don't care how long it takes. I'm saying as little as possible until one of them actually asks me what's wrong.

I'd tell you about the hotel, but I'm still pretty tired from all the sight-seeing. That's because Mom and Dad never take "vacations," they take "trips." On a trip there's a schedule where you have to see as much as possible, in as little time as possible, and you can never rest. I wish our family would take normal vacations, like a weekend in San Diego where you just lie on the beach the whole day, but Mom hates vacations like that. The last time we went to San Diego, Mom wouldn't go in the ocean because she didn't want to get her hair wet. Instead she took about five hours pinning her hair up, then she went to the hotel swimming pool and rented a kickboard so she could do leg exercises all day.

So this is definitely a trip. In just three days we've seen the

State Department, Ford's Theater, Watergate, the Treasury Department, the Commerce Department, and the Smithsonian Museum. I couldn't tell all the buildings apart after a while, so I took a bunch of brochures in case I felt like doing an extra credit report to make up for all the work I'm missing. But then I remembered how if you do too much extra credit at my school, they'll try to skip you ahead and ruin your life. That's why I figured I'd call Leslie instead.

Leslie said that Mr. Darlington gave us a pop quiz in history, and he also assigned a big research paper. It's due the Thursday after vacation, which means I'll only have four days to go to the library when I get back. Now I'll probably get a bad grade, and it's not even my fault. I mean, I can't help it if my parents won't let me go to school. Plus it gets even worse. Leslie said she danced with Chris for half a song at Erica's party, and I have to admit, Leslie's a really good dancer. She's the only girl I know who can shimmy and swing her hips like the eighth-grade girls do. Then I heard Tracy and Lana in the background, and Tracy told Leslie to stop wasting time talking to me. So I asked if I could talk to Lana, but Leslie said they had to go. "Go where?" I asked, but Leslie said it was a secret and she couldn't tell me over the phone. Then she hung up. She didn't even say she was sorry for stealing Chris from me. If I was allowed to stay home, this *never* would have happened.

After that, I wasn't planning on saying anything for the rest of my life, but it gets pretty boring not talking to anyone, so I did talk a little today. We had to get up early again because, like I said, Mom and Dad don't know how to relax. "We have a busy day planned," Mom said when she woke me up. Big surprise. She wouldn't even let me sleep through breakfast. I told her that even if she made me go down to breakfast, she couldn't make me eat. I said I'd rather sleep at the table than eat, I was so tired. But at breakfast, Mom ordered some cereal for me anyway. Naturally, she just drank black coffee and had about two bites of toast. Then I asked why I had to eat breakfast when Mom didn't, but Dad just said, "Don't start. We're planning on having a good day." The thing about my family is, you can never say anything that might ruin someone's day, even if you think it's very important. I was better off not talking.

After breakfast we went to the Supreme Court, the Capitol, the Library of Congress, and the National Archives. The only exciting part was when we saw the original Declaration of Independence in a glass case. It was pretty interesting so I read the whole thing, even though all the other tourists got mad at me for hogging up the view for so long. But I really liked what Thomas Jefferson was talking about, so I wouldn't move until I read the important parts over again. I mean, if everyone's supposed to be free in America, what about me? I told Mom and Dad that the Declaration of Independence was proof I should be able to stay in school if I wanted, or sleep late if I wanted, or skip breakfast if I wanted. I said I should be entitled to "life, liberty, and the pursuit of happiness," like Leslie and all my friends at home. It said so right there in the glass case. But Dad just told me to "grow up" and Mom acted like she didn't hear me. She was too busy looking at the Declaration of Independence and telling Dad how they should get writing like that on their next party invitations. I swear, she always misses the point.

When we got outside again, I saw this tall gray tower in the sky. It has no windows or doors, but wherever we went, I could see it above all the other buildings. I asked one of the tour guides what the tower was, and he told me it's the Washington Monument. Then he wouldn't stop talking about it, even though I only wanted to know its name. It sounded pretty interesting, though, so whenever I decided to talk, I kept asking Mom and Dad if we could visit the Washington Monument. I couldn't wait to go there because I thought it was neat how there's a building so tall and skinny with nothing in it. According to the tour guide, it's totally empty inside, except for a staircase and an elevator. Plus it doesn't blend in with the rest of the buildings. But Mom and Dad said we can't go there until it's on their schedule. I'm telling you, my parents haven't done a spontaneous thing in their lives.

Actually, one spontaneous thing happened out in the park, under some cherry trees. We were in between tours and since there were all these squirrels running around, Mom stopped to feed them. We already had lunch, but David was carrying around this giant tub of buttered popcorn we bought from a guy on the street, and that's what Mom used to feed the squirrels. It was sort of fun to watch at first, but then the squirrels started spitting out bits of popcorn and you could tell it was making them sick. They probably wanted nuts instead. So I told Mom to stop, but she kept wanting to get her picture taken while she was feeding the squirrels. Another thing about Mom is that she's crazy about pictures of herself. We have a picture of Mom smiling in front of every single building, museum, hotel, or restaurant we've ever visited.

So Mom kept feeding the poor squirrels while Dad snapped the pictures. Most of the squirrels still took the popcorn, but you could tell it was hard for them to swallow. I even saw one squirrel throw up on a tree trunk. I tried telling Mom that the squirrels weren't hungry anymore, but she wouldn't stop smiling at the camera and giving them more popcorn, like she was doing a popcorn commercial or something. Then she asked David and me to get in the picture and feed the squirrels with her, but I wasn't about to go make a bunch of squirrels eat if they didn't want to. Since David always does whatever Mom wants, though, David and Mom posed for the camera until the film finally ran out. So that's the most spontaneous thing we've done on this trip: feeding the squirrels until they puked.

# "That's My Girl"

Naturally, we had to get up early again today to stay on Mom and Dad's schedule. But I took a long time getting out of bed, so Mom told David to wait for me to shower before meeting them downstairs for breakfast. Which was fine with me, because I got to play tag with David in the hotel hallways. But on the way down, something terrible happened. I tried tagging David when we were running into the elevator, and the door closed on me and snagged my pants. The pants are part of this brand-new corduroy outfit I was supposed to wear to meet Dad's cousins for dinner. Even though Mom never noticed when I stopped talking, I knew she'd notice a snag on a new outfit.

But luckily, when we got to the restaurant, Mom didn't notice the snag because she was busy looking at the chubby lady sitting at the next table. The lady was ordering pancakes and sausage, with extra syrup, and David said he didn't think she needed the extra syrup. That made Mom and Dad laugh, but no one laughed when Dad and David also ordered pancakes and sausage with extra syrup. Then Mom ordered black coffee and a piece of toast and said she'd taste David and Dad's pancakes. I

swear, she's always either tasting other people's meals or dump-
ing her food on their plates. I don't know why she doesn't just
order what she wants in the first place.


When we finally got to Dad's cousins' house for dinner, I found
out that my cousin Kate and her mom do the tasting thing, too.
Kate's the daughter of Dad's cousin, Lou, who's a very smart
doctor but also likes to brag a lot. I heard Dad tell Mom that he
thinks Lou's pompous, which means he's conceited, but at
least Kate seemed nice. She's four years older than me, and she
wears all these grown-up clothes. Kate's mom said Kate used to
be a loudmouth, but lately she's matured a lot. Then Lou got
pompous and started bragging about how pretty Kate is and
how popular she is with the boys. He even called Kate a "little
lady," then he put his arm around her and smiled like mad. It
was pretty disgusting.

I kind of wondered if Kate would become a doctor like her
dad one day, but when I asked her about it, she said she used to
think about it sometimes, but now she wants to have a family
when she grows up. I almost couldn't hear what she said,
though, because she talks so quiet, like she's whispering secrets
to everyone. I couldn't imagine anyone ever calling her a loudmouth. But Lou said she wasn't really a loudmouth, exactly,
she was just too "spirited." "What's wrong with that?" I asked,
but then everyone laughed at me. I swear, people are always
laughing when I ask questions. That's why I never get any answers.

The whole time we were talking, we were sitting around in
the living room while Mom kept posing for pictures and asking
Dad to take a second shot, in case she blinked when the flash
went off. She said she wanted a picture of everyone there, but of
course, *she* had to be in all the pictures with everyone. I didn't
want to be in any of the pictures because I felt ugly standing

next to Kate. Kate's so much taller and thinner than me. She's like a real woman.

Mom finally ran out of film in her camera, thank God, so we all went into the dining room for dinner. That's when I found out that I also eat much more than Kate does. Kate and her mom took tiny helpings of everything, and just like Mom does with Dad and David, they said they'd taste Lou's dinner. I wasn't about to go tasting someone else's dinner, though, so I took normal helpings. That's when Kate said, "You must be really hungry," but she didn't say that to David even though he took the same amount of food I did. "You must be really full," I answered, since all Kate had on her plate was a small piece of chicken and a spoonful of rice. But then Kate's mom laughed again, even though I wasn't trying to be funny. I wish everyone would stop laughing at me for once.

Since Kate and her mom ate hardly any dinner, I figured they'd definitely eat dessert. Kate's mom bought three different desserts. One was this fudgy-looking chocolate cake, one was some disgusting lemon thing, and one was a cheesecake. Kate's mom stood at the head of the table and asked my dad which desserts he wanted. Dad said, "Some of all of them, please." Dad's skinny as a stick, but he loves dessert. Then it was David's turn, and he also asked for all three, even though he's not as skinny as Dad. So did Lou, except he said it in this really pompous tone, like you were supposed to already *know* he'd want all three.

Next it was Mom's turn. She said she'd have a tiny sliver of the chocolate cake, and she'd taste Dad's lemon tart and cheesecake. Big surprise. When it was my turn, I said I'd have some of the chocolate cake and some of the cheesecake. Kate said she didn't want anything because she was too full. Then Kate's mom sat down, but she didn't take any dessert either. She just brought in two clean forks for her and Kate so they could both taste Lou's desserts.

Then we all talked about how great the chocolate cake was, and Kate's mom said it was her favorite cake in the world because it came from the best bakery in town. So I asked why she wasn't having any if she loved it so much. "I want to maintain my girl-ish figure," she said, then she winked at Lou. "That's my girl," Lou answered, and he winked, too. At first I thought Lou was talking about Kate, since *she's* his girl, but then he gave his wife one of those really phony romantic kisses, just to show everyone how madly in love they are after all these years. I almost puked.

So I guess here's another rule: If you're a woman, you're supposed to try to look like a girl with a "girlish figure." But if you're a girl, you're supposed to act like a woman by not being "spirited." Except I eat and talk like the guys do. No wonder everyone thinks I'm a weirdo.

Before we left, Dad wanted me to write down Kate's address so I can send her pen pal letters when I get back home. I said I would, partly because I like to write, and partly because, other than my bird, Chrissy, I probably won't have any friends left to talk to when I get home anyway. I mean, I might get lonely. Then right when we were getting in the car, Mom finally no-ticed the snag in my pants. "What's that?" she asked, but be-fore I could think of anything to say, Mom said she'd take my pants to the concierge the minute we got back so he could get them fixed. She didn't even get mad, but that's because she was proud of how I acted at the pompous cousins' house. She said I acted "like a lady" tonight, probably because I'm still not talk-ing very much. Mom said I could learn a lot from Kate.

But then I asked Mom if she thought Kate's mom would stand over their kitchen sink later tonight and stuff some of that chocolate cake she loves so much into her mouth. That's when Mom said I wasn't being ladylike anymore. But if you want my opinion, I'll bet Lou would be pretty surprised to see his "girl" stuffing her face with chocolate cake in the middle of the night. Maybe then he wouldn't be so pompous.

When we got back to the hotel, I went into the bathroom to take off the snagged pants. The snag was on the back, and when I looked in the mirror I noticed that my butt looked big compared to Kate's. So I got on the scale and found out that I weigh 69 pounds. I'm not sure if that's good or not. Normally the only time I ever get weighed is when I go to the doctor for my checkup every birthday, so usually I don't think about my weight during the rest of the year. But I guess I got curious because Kate told me she weighs 95 pounds, even though all of Mom's friends think your weight is supposed to be private information. Believe me, Mom's friends would rather admit how old they are before they'll tell you their weight, and they always lie like mad about that. But Kate loved talking about her weight. She said she used to weigh 105 pounds because she was studying all the time and didn't get much exercise. But now she takes dance instead of science club after school, and whenever there's stairs and an elevator, she always takes the stairs. That's how she got so popular.

I asked Kate if she also lost weight from not eating very much, but Kate said she's not on a diet. Which made no sense, since she hardly ate anything at dinner. Then Kate explained how that's not a diet, it's just how you have to eat when you grow up. I told Kate it sure sounded like a diet to me, and I wanted to know how long it takes before you can eat normal-sized meals again. "Like a year, or five years?" I asked, but Kate didn't know. "I guess never," she answered. Then she told me to be sure to take the stairs instead of the elevator when we visit the Washington Monument tomorrow.

# The Lori Monument

I didn't want to get cramps or anything climbing up the stairs at the Washington Monument, so I didn't eat much at breakfast. That's because I remembered that one of Julie's mom's diet books said you're supposed to allow at least three hours for your food to digest before you exercise, and I really wanted to prove to Kate that I could climb to the top. But then I found out that we weren't going to the Washington Monument until 3:00, so I didn't eat much lunch either.

At the restaurant, though, Mom and Dad saw I wasn't eating and told me I had to have something. In case you haven't noticed, my parents get stuck on very weird things sometimes. They didn't care when I wouldn't *talk* for a week, but they sure cared if I *ate* today. They cared so much they said we wouldn't leave the restaurant until I ate something, since I didn't eat any breakfast either. I couldn't believe it! So when the waitress came by and asked if she could take my plate, I said I was finished, but Dad told her to leave it there. He said it in his Walter Cronkite voice, too, which made the people at the next table look over. They probably thought Dad was a famous newscaster or something.

"She's still working on her lunch," Dad said. I swear, the

whole restaurant heard. Then the waitress asked Mom if she was finished, and I answered, "No, she's still working on her lunch, too," but Mom glared at me and told the waitress she was done. "Then I'm done, too," I said, which pretty much confused the waitress. She started to take my plate again, but when Dad said, "No you aren't, young lady," the waitress got out of there pretty fast. She practically ran, but I don't blame her or anything. Trust me, you don't exactly want to hang around with Dad when he's mad.

After that we just sat there, and I kept trying to concentrate on my napkin so I wouldn't have to eat. The restaurant had these really big napkins, the kind you can fold into birds and hats and things, so I was making a paper bird and deciding if I wanted to stop talking again. But I didn't want to miss getting to the Washington Monument, and I couldn't eat because I didn't want to take any chances of getting cramps and not making it to the top. So I tried talking to Dad because he loves logical arguments so much. I told him that he let the waitress take Mom's plate away even though she didn't eat anything either. But then Mom butted in and said she did eat—she ate a salad. That's when I said I'd eat four bites of salad for lunch, just like Mom did, but she said I can't eat like that until I'm a little bit older.

That's when Mom opened up her big purse. I thought she might start crying and that she was reaching for some tissues, but instead she took out a stack of postcards and started writing. Mom's as big on postcards as she is on pictures. She sends all her friends postcards from every single trip, even if she'll be home before the postcards get there. And they all say exactly the same thing:

Dear (Boring Person),
(Whatever stupid city we're in) is marvelous!! We're having an absolutely lovely time!! Our hotel is wonderful, and the sights are breathtaking!! We went to see (names of hundreds

of boring buildings). The people are all so darling, and the shopping is fabulous!! We can't wait to show you our pictures when we get back!

Much love to (names of boring family members).

Love, The Gottliebs. XOXO

I think Mom should just have them preprinted before every trip, like those *Mad Libs* we do at recess, where you fill in all the blanks. There could be blanks for things like city, building, museum, shopping area, and person's name, and then she could send out millions of postcards at once. I mean, it would sure save a lot of time on her schedule.

Anyway, Mom was writing a postcard to Erica's mom, but I was getting scared that if we sat there too long, the Washington Monument might close. So I told Dad I didn't feel good, and that's why I wasn't eating. I even put my hand on my stomach and tried to make my face look sick, but I guess Dad didn't believe me. He said if I was too sick to eat, I was also too sick to go to the Washington Monument. Then I tried explaining that I wasn't sick with the *flu* or anything, I just didn't feel good.

That's when Dad's vein started popping out. Dad has this big vein in his forehead that always pops out when he loses his temper, and the last time I saw it was after I yelled the F-word. He was so mad his lip started shaking, too. Boy, if I knew my parents would pay so much attention to me if I skipped two meals, I would've done *that* instead of not talking for a week. Maybe then I could have stayed home from Washington.

"Goddamnit, Lori Ellen, eat your sandwich right now," Dad said. It scared me seeing Dad's lip shaking, so I looked down at my lap. The weird thing is, my legs looked kind of fat when they were uncrossed. I never noticed that before. But then I crossed them and they looked thin again. Maybe that's why ladies are crossing their legs all the time. "Look at me when I'm talking to you," I heard Dad say, but I knew all I'd see if I looked up was that gross vein on Dad's forehead, so I just kept staring at my legs and trying to figure out why they looked so much skinnier when they were crossed. "If you don't listen to me and eat your lunch, you're going to be very sorry later on," Dad said. I wasn't sure what that was supposed to mean, since nothing could make me sorrier than being trapped in some restaurant in Washington and missing everything at school. But I still wouldn't look up. I was peeking over at Mom's lap where she was writing her phony postcards, and she was writing the part about what an "absolutely lovely" time we were all having. Then I felt sick for real.

That's when I heard Dad's voice again, only this time it was shaking like his lip was. "Okay, that's it. You're not going to the Washington Monument, and when we get back home, you're grounded. No friends after school for two weeks." Like I even have any friends anymore. But then the nicest voice you've ever heard in your entire life said, "Waitress, could we have the check, please?" Dad can switch from Walter Cronkite to Mr. Rogers pretty quick.

When we finally got outside, Mom and Dad ignored me again like they always do when I make them mad. Except I sort of didn't care for once. I'm serious. I usually care a lot, but I guess I was happy that I didn't have to eat anything if I didn't want to. I mean, I was hungry, but it felt neat, like I was *flying* or something. My whole body felt empty inside, just like the Washington Monument. I kind of liked it, which is why I didn't eat much at dinner, even though the Washington Monument was already closed. And besides, it doesn't matter that I never climbed to the top, because if I stop eating from now on, I can still make my legs look as skinny as Kate's. One of Julie's mom's diet books said that if you diet enough you'll never need to exercise. You just can't eat very much, that's all.

# Sorry About the Milk Shake, Mr. President

The way I figured it, if you're planning on skipping a meal, breakfast is probably the easiest one to miss if you sleep late enough. First of all, you can't be hungry when you're asleep, unless you *dream* about food, and second of all, I didn't want to get in another fight with Mom and Dad about eating. I knew if I told them I didn't feel like eating, they'd tell me I was being ridiculous. If it's their idea, it's never ridiculous, but if it's something I want to do, that's *always* ridiculous.

So when the alarm went off this morning, I told David to tell Mom I had a fever, because usually you have to have something serious like a fever for people to stop bugging you. David said he knew I didn't have a fever, but I scrunched up my face and gave him our special funny look, which made him laugh, so he agreed to tell Mom for me anyway. I'm a pretty bad liar, but then I remembered what I read in the magazine where they interviewed the actress with the big boobs who sang the "Tits and Ass" song in *A Chorus Line.* The actress kept saying how she uses a very serious method when she's acting, and that's why she's such a wonderful actress. She was pretty conceited, obviously. It turns out that her whole method is that she tricks herself into believing she's someone else. Then she's not acting anymore, she's just being herself. Sometimes she even becomes the *thing* she's singing about. I kind of wondered what she felt like being a tit and an ass.

Anyway, when I was trying to lie today, I closed my eyes and tried to become a sick eleven-year-old girl with a scratchy, red throat and a terrible fever that makes you shiver even when you're under all the covers. I didn't know if I could do it at first, but I guess becoming a sick kid is a lot easier than becoming a tit, because by the time Mom came in, I almost started believing I really *was* sick. I even thought I was getting away with my first lie ever because I heard Mom tell Dad that they should let me sleep while they went down to breakfast. Dad said I was just playing games, though, and that "enough is enough," another of his favorite expressions. But Mom ended up telling Dad to just let it go. I was glad Mom stuck up for me for once, but I wasn't exactly thrilled about the way she did it. She said that I would just "aggravate" everyone over breakfast and for their own "sanity" they should let me sleep.


I have to admit, skipping breakfast wasn't the best idea I've ever had. I hardly ate anything yesterday, and because we were scheduled for a 1:00 tour of the White House, we wouldn't be eating lunch until at least 2:30. So by 12:30, after spending hours shopping for tacky souvenirs with Mom, I felt kind of dizzy. I guess I was sort of lagging behind when we were walking over to the White House, because Dad said he knew I shouldn't have skipped breakfast, and he hoped I learned my lesson. That's another thing Dad loves to say: "I hope you learned your lesson, young lady." Dad thought I should eat something before the tour, but I said I wasn't *hungry,* I was just *tired,* and that's why I was lagging behind. The minute I said it, though, I knew it wasn't logical enough for Dad.

"We let you sleep late this morning so you wouldn't be tired," he said. You always have to be careful when you lie to Dad because you can't have any holes in your story. But Dad didn't seem to care this time, because then we passed a Baskin-Robbins and Mom wanted to go in. She said that David might want some ice cream, which really meant she'd taste whatever he got. Mom never eats anything at meals, but I'm telling you, she has radar for junk food.

Even though part of me didn't want to, I ended up ordering a milk shake. I would have gotten only a small cup of ice cream, but Dad said we didn't have time for me to sit down and eat, and they wouldn't allow any food in the White House. I could drink a milk shake on the way over. I got double chocolate and it tasted so great I took a long time sipping it. Then Dad said I had to finish the entire milk shake before we got to the White House, and that I wasn't allowed to skip breakfast anymore. "Your mother and I are putting an end to your ridiculous game," he said.

I never finished the milk shake, though, because when we got to the White House, this girl Donna Landers was standing in line with her family for the same tour we were supposed to go on, and I almost had a heart attack! I wanted David to hide me, but he didn't know who Donna was.

I told David about how Donna Landers is the most popular girl at another school in my district, and she's friends with Leslie. Except she's the nastiest girl our age. She's so nasty she doesn't even bother talking about you behind your back like the other popular girls do. She'll actually insult you to your face, but everyone in my grade would kill to be Donna's friend anyway. Not me, though. I'd never be friends with her, no matter what.

The trouble started when my parents heard me telling David

about Donna. Mom thought Donna was "absolutely adorable" and Dad said it was such a coincidence that someone I knew from home was on the same White House tour. "It's such a small world," Dad kept saying over and over, like he was a famous philosopher or something. "It really is," Mom answered. I was thinking that the world was way too small, if you asked me, but then Mom and Dad both repeated how small the world was.

Finally, Mom told me to go say hi to Donna, but since I would rather have eaten breakfast than talk to her, I told Mom I didn't even know her. It's true, I only know who she is. But things got worse, anyway, if that's even possible. Dad mentioned again what a coincidence seeing the Landers family was, and that made Mom say, "Isn't this fun? Let's go introduce ourselves." Fun my butt. I begged them not to, but Mom told me to keep my voice down, and before I knew it, Mom and Dad were walking over to the Landers! The tour was just starting and I tried to hide behind some other families, but it was too late. I could tell that something awful was about to happen.

We were at the entrance to the White House, and Mom, Dad, and David were off having an entire conversation with the Landers family. I heard Mom tell Donna's mom that "our daughters know each other," even though I just said I didn't know Donna. But Donna acted like she had no idea who I was either, because my parents were pointing at me and Donna was shaking her head with her eyes closed, like she might fall asleep any second. Donna always acts like everyone else is way too boring for her. Finally the tour guide started talking and my family came back.

That's when Dad noticed I still had the milk shake with me. Before the tour started, we walked past a huge sign that said, ABSOLUTELY NO FOOD OR DRINKS PERMITTED. USE OF CAMERAS PROHIBITED, and I stuffed the milk shake under my coat. I had to because there were security guards everywhere, even though they were wearing plain suits so they'd look like regular people who just happen to carry around walkie-talkies all the time. They weren't fooling anyone, especially me, so I was pretty careful about hiding the milk shake at first. But I guess I forgot about hiding it when this thing with Donna Landers happened.

When Dad saw the milk shake, he got mad at me, partly for bringing it inside, but mostly for not drinking the whole thing. Then he told me that when we got outside again, we weren't going anywhere until I finished the entire milk shake. End of discussion, naturally. I figured if I had to drink the whole thing, I wouldn't eat lunch. I mean, I sort of hated myself for getting it in the first place. I knew Kate would never have even a sip of a milk shake, no matter how hungry she got. Donna probably wouldn't either. You should see how skinny her legs are.

I didn't really *want* to do what I did next, but there was no way I was planning on sitting outside the White House and arguing in front of Donna Landers about drinking a stupid milk shake. So my first plan was to say I had to go to the bathroom so I could pour the milk shake down a toilet. Since I didn't see any lady Secret Service people, I figured the ladies' bathroom would be pretty safe. But then I figured Mom would probably want to come along because she and all her friends love going to the ladies' room so they can put on more lipstick. So my next plan was to spill out a little bit at a time as we walked so no one would notice until later, when they found the tiny brown stains on the carpets. But I didn't want to mess up the whole White House, and besides, I just don't think you should go ruining all the president's rugs if you're visiting his house. That's when I noticed I was standing next to a big bookcase. Mom, Dad, and David were over with the Landers again, and I was crammed in behind a bunch of people. No one could see me because I'm pretty short.

That gave me an idea. I didn't have time to think about what I was doing since we never spent much time in any of the rooms. They kept rushing us around everywhere, I guess be-

cause the tour guides can't memorize very much information.
So all of a sudden, I opened up my coat and dumped the rest of
the chocolate milk shake into the bookcase! Then the whole
tour moved on. I swear, no one even noticed. I didn't think
messing up a single bookcase was as bad as messing up all the
carpets, but I still looked to see if I ruined any important
books. They all looked like decoration, though. I doubt
anyone's planning on actually reading them.

When the tour finally ended, Dad told me that we weren't
going anywhere until I drank the entire milk shake, but I told
him I already drank it inside. Then I handed him the empty
container to prove it. But since Dad's a very suspicious person,
he wanted to know how I could have finished the milk shake
with all the security people around. I just sort of shrugged and
told him no one seemed to care. "Besides," I said, "what could
I possibly have done with it in the White House? I mean, really,
Dad." He couldn't argue with that.

We had lunch at this neat restaurant that played jazz music
and had plants hanging all over the place. I already decided it
would be okay to eat part of a sandwich since I didn't drink the
rest of the milk shake. But when I ordered the sandwich, it also
came with potato salad. I guess Kate forgot about telling me to
always read the fine print on menus.

I figured that eating half of the sandwich would be enough to
make Mom and Dad happy, but Dad said I had to eat some
potato salad, too. I told Dad that Mom didn't eat her potato
salad either, she just dumped it onto Dad's plate. I said I
wished I could also just dump my food onto someone else's
plate if I didn't feel like eating it, like Mom did. But then Mom
said, "We won't keep having this struggle with you while we're
trying to enjoy our vacation." There was no way I was eating
those potatoes.

According to the schedule, we were supposed to be at Dad's

Uncle Morris and Aunt Rose's apartment by 4:00, because David and I are staying there for a few days so Mom and Dad can' go out alone. So I looked at my watch to see how close it was to 4:00. That's when I noticed my wrists looked skinny, just like Kate's. I figured maybe not eating was working after all. The best part was, it was already 3:30, and Mom and Dad hate being late. I knew I'd win the argument. I made three rabbits and a sailor's hat out of my napkin before Mom and Dad finally gave in.

After we left the restaurant, Mom, Dad, and David walked ahead of me again, and I followed behind like their stray cat or something. Then Mom stopped by a mailbox to send more postcards, and Dad and David had a whole conversation about American history. No one said anything to me, so I just made sure not to step on any lines on the sidewalk. But right when we got to Uncle Morris and Aunt Rose's door, Dad turned around to where I was standing. "You better not play this game at Morris and Rose's," he said in his shaky voice. I figured he was done talking because usually Dad doesn't say much when his voice starts shaking. But all of a sudden he said, "If you give them any trouble, I swear, I'll kill you." I started to say something back—like how eating small meals isn't worth being *murdered* over—but Dad butted in and said, "End of discussion." Even though we weren't having a discussion in the first place.

# Day of Atonement

Dad may love ending discussions, but he sure won't end the discussion about what I eat. He even brought it up again last night when Mom and Dad got back from dinner with the pompous cousins. The reason it came up was because Dad's Uncle Morris and Aunt Rose are pretty old, so all they talk about is food. Right away they mentioned that I didn't eat much at dinner while Mom and Dad were out at the restaurant.

Aunt Rose said that David "ate like a horse." "The boy's such a good eater," she said. But then she said that "the little one"—that was me—"ate like a bird." She loved comparing us to animals. "She was just tired," Aunt Rose went on, "but the girl needs to get some meat on her bones. The boy, he's healthy as an ox."

After Uncle Morris and Aunt Rose went into their bedroom, Mom and Dad came to say good night to David and me before they went back to their hotel. Dad told me again how I was just going to have to eat, like I'd say, "Okay, Dad. I love you," and then we'd all hug and go to sleep. They do that on *The Brady Bunch* all the time, but that's never happened in my family. Not once. What really happened was, I said, "You can't make me," which got Mom pretty mad. "Oh yes, we can," she said. "Oh no, you can't," I answered. "We certainly can," Mom said again. "Yeah, how?" I asked. I mean, what were they gonna do, make me sit in a Baskin-Robbins until I drank ten thousand milk shakes? "We just can," Mom answered. Like I told you, Mom hates explaining things.

Finally Dad chimed in. I figured he'd just say, "End of discussion," and walk out, but instead he said, "You might think you can play this game forever, but we won't ignore your behavior." That's when I knew I had the most logical argument ever! I told Dad that the more he pays attention to what I eat, the less I'll eat. Then I told him that if he'd just *ignore* what I eat, everything would be fine. "You ignored me when I stopped talking for a week, and see, I'm talking again," I said.

Then I don't know why, but right after I said that, I felt really sad. I sort of wanted Mom to come over and hug me, like Mrs. Brady would do if Marcia or Jan or Cindy was sad about something. That's when the weirdest thing happened: Mom turned into Florence Henderson! It was like *magic*. She got up from her chair, walked over to my bed, and kissed me good night on my forehead. "Sleep tight, honey," she said, then Mom and Dad left. It was a weird thing for Mom to do anyway, but it was even weirder because usually Mom doesn't like it when my argument makes more sense than Dad's.

I didn't see Mom and Dad at all this morning. The good thing about staying with Dad's Uncle Morris and Aunt Rose is that we can just relax in the apartment all day while Mom and Dad go around snapping pictures and visiting more boring buildings. The only problem is that the apartment smells like medicine, and all the sofas are covered in plastic, so you have to sit on sofas that stick to your legs when you get up. Plus Aunt Rose spends all day talking about food.

Unlike Mom, Aunt Rose doesn't have a housekeeper, so she

actually makes all the food herself. Lunch was a half grapefruit, some cheesy casserole thing, and homemade bread on the side. It smelled pretty good compared to the apartment smell, and since I slept through breakfast today, I could have eaten a little bit extra. I also could have eaten extra because when I went into the bathroom to take a shower, I was looking under the sink for some soap and I found a scale. I was kind of surprised because I didn't think old people cared if they looked sexy or not. I also found Uncle Morris's teeth in a plastic jar, which was pretty gross. Anyway, it turns out I weigh 65 pounds, four pounds less than I weighed on the hotel scale. But I think something's wrong with their scale because my legs still look fat if they're not crossed.

That's why when I sat down at lunch, I got scared I might get fat from smelling the food. I could see the steam rising up from the casserole, and I remembered from science class that the steam has to go somewhere, and it would probably stay somewhere in the apartment since all the windows were closed because of the rain. Then I figured the steam must be going right up my nose, into my body, and straight to my stomach. I felt pretty full all of a sudden.

I was way too full to eat anything, but Aunt Rose gets sensitive if people don't eat her food. So during the whole meal, Aunt Rose would point at the casserole or the bread and say, "*Es kinder,*" which I found out means "Eat, children," in Yiddish. David explained that when Uncle Morris and Aunt Rose grew up, they didn't have a lot of food around, so they kept making sure we got enough to eat. That's why Aunt Rose went back into the kitchen and came out with all kinds of things she said she'd make for me—sandwiches, soup, cookies, you name it. But each time I shook my head no, Uncle Morris and Aunt Rose would say something to each other in Yiddish, then Aunt Rose would go back into the kitchen and bring out even *more* foods to choose from. She's a really nice lady, but I just couldn't get her to understand that she could bring me the best meal in the universe and I still wouldn't eat it. No offense to her or anything.

Aunt Rose looked pretty sad, though, so finally I ate a few bites of the grapefruit. I figured it couldn't be that fattening. But it tasted sweeter than I expected, and that's when I saw the bowl of sugar on the table. It turned out that Aunt Rose already sprinkled a little sugar on the cut grapefruit halves to make them taste better, but I didn't want any sugar. "Sugar is the enemy," one of Julie's mom's diet books said. Then in big letters it said, "ALWAYS AVOID SUGAR!" which Julie cut out of the book and pinned on the wall in her bedroom. I couldn't think about Julie's mom's diet book and eat the grapefruit at the same time, so I stopped eating.

That's when Uncle Morris and Aunt Rose started whispering in Yiddish again and looking over at me every few sentences. They kept asking if I was sick, or if I needed anything, or if there was something else Aunt Rose could make for me. I wanted to say something to make Aunt Rose feel better about her cooking, but I obviously couldn't eat with all that steam going into my stomach. So finally I told her that I was fasting, like on the Yom Kippur holiday, because I was trying to learn more about my religion. The truth is, my family isn't too religious, but I thought it was a pretty good lie to come up with so fast. Then Uncle Morris tried explaining that the Yom Kippur holiday is in September, not April, that the fast lasts only one day, until sundown, and that the whole point of the fast is to atone for your sins. "A sweet girl like you?" he said. "Surely you have no sins to atone for." Talk about making me feel terrible for lying.

But lying made things worse, if that's even possible, because Aunt Rose got excited and said she'd make a wonderful dinner for me, a tradition on Yom Kippur when the fast ends. I promised God that if Aunt Rose would forget about making me this huge dinner, I'd never lie again. I meant it, too, and I don't even believe in God all the time. But I guess God knew about me not believing in Him, because Aunt Rose wouldn't stop talking about the dinner she was planning on making me. Then David gave me a look that meant "Busted!" and I gave him my nastiest glare back, so he mouthed "Busted" at me and smiled really wide. David loves it when I get in trouble lately.

For the rest of the day I tried keeping my mind off getting in trouble. I wrote my first letter to Kate, since we're leaving the day after tomorrow and I won't see her again. I told her that I never climbed the stairs at the Washington Monument, but it's okay because I'm eating like her now. Then I asked Uncle Morris to lick the postage stamp, just in case you could get fat from the glue they use. I mean, you never know what people put in things, like the sugar on the grapefruit. I wonder if Kate will lick the postage stamp when she writes me back, but I doubt it. People like Kate probably never lick postage stamps.

When Mom and Dad finally came back to the apartment around dinnertime, Mom had tears running down her face and her makeup was smeared because they came from their last visit with the pompous cousins. Mom always cries for hours when she says good-bye to people, but tonight she sure stopped crying fast. That's because she found Aunt Rose busy in the kitchen making my "break the fast" dinner. Then she went berserk. I'm serious.

Mom yelled that I was embarrassing, selfish, crazy, and some other things I can't remember right now. She was screaming so loud she was practically breaking my eardrums. The worst part was, she said she wouldn't love me if I wasn't her daughter. "I hate you!" she screamed. Then I sort of whispered that I hated her, too, but that made her start crying again. So I said I didn't hate *her,* I just hated it when she screamed at me at the top of her lungs. It's true, I don't hate *her.* I mean, she's my mom. I really hoped she would take back what she said about me, since I took back what I said about her, but she never did. She just went off to find some tissues in her big purse.

The minute Mom left, Dad came running into the room. It was like a relay race where you hand off the baton to the next person. Except Dad didn't say he wouldn't love me if I wasn't his daughter. He was mad because he thought I was being "horrible" to Uncle Morris and Aunt Rose, but I wasn't trying to be horrible to them. I mean, they're the only people who've been nice to me lately.

Finally Dad said that when we get back to L.A., Mom's taking me to see Mayo Katz so he can put an end to my game. Mayo's my pediatrician and he's also one of Mom and Dad's friends. David and I always call Mayo "Mayonnaise" because when we were little we thought Mayo was such a funny name. Julie once heard us calling him that, and said she'd hate to be called Mayonnaise because it's the grossest food there is. It has 100 calories in just one tablespoon. That's why she isn't allowed to have any mayonnaise on her turkey sandwiches.

Anyway, when everyone was finally done yelling at me, I went back into the bedroom. David looked like he was taking a nap, but I knew he was faking because he couldn't possibly have slept through all that racket. "They're making me go see Mayonnaise," I said, and David opened his eyes and answered, "I know." I started crying a little, but then David gave me our funny look to try to cheer me up. I could tell he felt bad about everything that happened. "I don't want to go to Mayonnaise," I told David, but right after I said "Mayonnaise," I whispered "Dr. Katz," kind of like the way I whisper "A" if I say "be" by accident. From now on, I'm calling him "Dr. Katz."

# 2:
## Spring 1978

# Please Help the Hungry

The second we got home from Washington, Mom got on the phone and made three appointments: one with her hair lady, one with her nail lady, and one with Dr. Katz. I told Mom I didn't need to go a doctor for trying to eat like a normal woman, but then Mom gave Dad her nervous look. That made Dad go into his study to smoke his pipe and Mom go into the bedroom, probably to read one of her *Redbook* magazines or organize her closet for the millionth time.

There weren't any *Redbook*s in Dr. Katz's waiting room today. The magazines were mostly things like *Highlights for Children,* but there was also a *Bon Appétit* which I started reading. The whole magazine, even the ads, was about food. Mom's magazines have recipes in them, too—like "12 Great Cookie Ideas"—but then on the next page they always have articles called "12 Great Diet Plans" that tell you never to eat what you just baked. In *Bon Appétit,* you're actually allowed to eat what you bake. Plus it doesn't tell you how many calories all the recipes have, like Mom's magazines do.

I know a lot about calories because on Monday, when I was walking home with Julie, we went into the bookstore and I bought a bunch of diet books with all the allowance money I'd saved up. One of them is called *My Calorie-Counting Companion,* and it lists the number of calories in every food in the universe. The reason it's called your "companion" is because you're supposed to carry it with you everywhere you go, just in case you suddenly need to look up how many calories something has. It's a pretty good book if you only read the part that lists the calories, but don't bother reading the part that talks about how to diet. It says things like, "If you take in fewer calories than you burn up each day, you're bound to shed pounds." Duh.

Anyway, I didn't want Julie to know I was on a diet because she has a big mouth and might tell her mom, who has an even bigger mouth and might tell my mom, who has the biggest mouth of all and uses it to scream at me. So I told Julie the books were for my mom, as a present, and Julie helped me pick out the ones her mom likes best. But since her mom never loses any weight from reading those books, I bought only the ones Julie said her mom *didn't* have.

When I got home, I ran upstairs and hid the books under my mattress because that's how David hides his *Playboy* magazines, and I don't think Mom and Dad know about those. But I do. I once saw David take his *Playboy*s out from under his mattress and bring them into the bathroom with him. I keep planning on taking one of the magazines when David's not home, just to see what a sexy woman looks like, but I always chicken out. David said he'd kill me if I ever touched his things, and I have a feeling he meant it. But since David reads his *Playboy*s in the bathroom, I figured the bathroom must be a pretty private place to read my diet books, too.

I'm a very fast reader, so I've learned a lot about diets in just a few days. All the books say that if you want to lose weight, you have to be very committed and you have to follow their rules. The only trouble is, each book has different rules. Like one book says you have to put water in whatever you're drinking so there's less of it, another book says you have to put your fork down between every bite, and another book says you have to cut all your meals in half when you sit down to eat, in fourths if you're in a restaurant, because everyone in America eats too much. I'm telling you, I've learned so many rules since I turned eleven that I can't keep track of them all.

One book says that if you follow their rules—like drinking three full glasses of water one hour before every meal to fill yourself up—you'll lose a pound a day, and all your friends will be jealous of you. Another book says that once you start losing weight, everyone will ask, "How did you do it?" but you shouldn't tell them because it's "your little secret." Then right above that part it says, "*New York Times* bestseller." Some secret. They're pretty phony books, obviously, but at least I have a plan.

So I was trying to figure out what I wouldn't eat at dinner when Dr. Katz's nurse called Mom and me into the examination room. I sat on one of those tables covered with crinkly white paper, and Dr. Katz asked, "What can I do for you, darlin'?" Dr. Katz is from Texas and he always sounds really cheery, even when you have a sore throat.

Before I could answer, though, Mom gave Dr. Katz a long speech about how I purposely ruined the trip to Washington, and how she has no idea what I'm up to this time, but she's tired of all the games I'm playing. "We thought you could knock some sense into her," she said. Like he could take the little hammer he uses to test my reflexes, tap me on the head a few times, and suddenly I'd start eating potato salad again.

Instead Dr. Katz took some blood. "Squeeze tighter," Mom kept telling me. Mom doesn't like the sight of needles, so I always have to hold her hand when I get shots or have blood taken. Mom's so scared of this stuff that when Dr. Katz finally says, "Okay, it's over," I have to promise her the Band-Aid's on before she'll finally open her eyes and let go of my hand.

After taking the blood, Dr. Katz weighed me, listened to my heart and lungs, and shined a light down my throat even though I wasn't coughing or anything. That's because Dr. Katz gets a big kick out of using his tongue depressors. If you want my opinion, the whole reason he became a doctor in the first place is so he could use tongue depressors all day. But when nothing was wrong with me, he looked me right in the eye for about twenty minutes without saying a word. Finally Dr. Katz asked why I lost six pounds since my last check-up in December. I tried telling him that I didn't know why I lost weight, but Mom kept butting in and saying, "Oh, please" every second.

I told Dr. Katz that Mom and Dad are making a big deal over nothing ("Oh, please"), that since he's a doctor he should understand that people go through weight fluctuations (I learned about those from *You Can Have a Perfect Body*), and that I'm just trying to eat healthy because Mom keeps poisoning us with unhealthy foods like Wonder bread and mayonnaise ("Oh, please, Lori!"). I would have shown him the diet books to back up the part about Mom feeding us unhealthy foods, but I figured I'd just get punished for buying the books in the first place. I get punished for everything, in case you haven't noticed.

Then Dr. Katz said to go into his office so we could talk about my "situation." "What situation?" I asked. I mean, everyone else is watching what they eat, and *they're* not being sent to the pediatrician because of it. Dr. Katz didn't answer though. He just said that a girl my age should be gaining weight, not losing it; that I'm supposed to gain more weight than usual over the next few years because I'm starting to develop (into what—a fat person?); and that even though I've always been skinny, I'll start to develop curves that may feel "awkward" (which really means fat) at first. In order for this to happen, though, I need to follow a sensible diet, which, Dr. Katz said, "doesn't mean a reduction of calories." (That's not what *My Calorie-Counting Companion* says.) Then Dr. Katz told me I have to drink three eight-ounce glasses of whole milk each day, and to come back for a "weight check" in one week. Mrs. Rivers might be stupid, but she sure was right about life being unfair.

At the end of our appointment, Mom and Dr. Katz gave each other one of those phony hugs where you kiss the air behind the person's neck. Then Mom's eyes started tearing up and she wouldn't stop thanking Dr. Katz. "Thank you so much," she whispered over and over, like he just saved my life because he told me to drink whole milk. He obviously went to a very bad medical school. But Mom was so excited about Dr. Katz's plan that when we left, she drove straight to the market to buy whole milk so I'd have it for dinner. It was one thing to bug me about my diet, but this whole milk thing was going way too far. Only babies drink whole milk. Everyone keeps telling me to act like a lady, but they treat me like a baby! I swear, people are so mixed-up.

I didn't want to go to the market with Mom, especially since I was hungry and was scared to see all that food. I have to admit, since I came back from Washington, I haven't exactly been eating the lunches she packs for me. On Monday I ate half of my salami sandwich, left the other half in my desk, and gave away the Fritos to my friends who only had healthy food in their lunches. Then on Tuesday, I gave away the Fritos again, but I didn't want to eat any of the sandwich, and I couldn't keep leaving all that food in my desk because it would stink up the whole classroom. So I tried giving the sandwich away, too. Tracy took half, but only because Michael loves salami and it would give her an excuse to go over to his lunch table. No one wanted the rest, so I had to throw it away even though I felt bad because I always see those collection boxes in the market saying PLEASE HELP THE HUNGRY, with a picture of a starving kid on the poster.

I didn't like the idea of wasting food, but I knew it wouldn't be easy giving my lunch away every day. So today I just tossed the whole bag into a garbage can on my way into homeroom, then I went to the library at lunch. I thought I might read some diet books during the lunch period, but the librarian stopped me when I walked in. "You need to eat your lunch outside," she practically yelled. Librarians are always telling you to whisper, but believe me, they're the loudest people I've ever met in my life.

I didn't have a lunch with me, so I kept on walking over to a cubicle. That's when the librarian shouted, "There's no food or drinks allowed in the library!" Perfect, I wanted to say, because there's no food or drinks allowed in my body either. But our librarian doesn't have a very good sense of humor, so I told her I ate my lunch at the morning recess and I needed to work on a report. The truth is, it was making me hungry being around everyone else's food at lunchtime.


That's why I couldn't wait to get out of the market with Mom. But since Mom loves to shop—for *anything*—it took her a while to decide what to buy. She's not one of those moms who goes to the grocery store with a list either. Mom just pushes the cart up and down every single aisle and tosses in whatever looks good. Except every time she throws something fattening into the cart like ice cream or cookies, she says, "Dad will love this" or "David loves these" just so whoever might be listening in the grocery aisle won't think Mom's buying the food for herself. She doesn't think it's very ladylike to buy fattening foods for yourself. The only things Mom buys for herself are cottage cheese and tomatoes.

When we got to the dairy section, Mom went straight to the whole milk and put it in the cart. "This is for you, Lori," she said, so no one in the aisle would think it was for her. But I told

Mom it would be a waste to buy it because I wasn't planning on drinking it. I even tried explaining about those collection boxes and how all these kids are starving, and how she should take the money she was spending on the whole milk and put it in the collection box as charity. I figured Mom would like that idea because she loves dressing up and going to charity events all the time.

"You'll drink it because Dr. Katz told you to, and those are doctor's orders," she said. I told Mom that I don't care if he's a doctor, I'm not taking orders about food from someone with a turkey chin whose belly hangs over his pants. I mean, what could he possibly know about nutrition? But Mom just repeated that I have to follow doctor's orders.

When we got to the cereal aisle, Mom started putting sugary cereals like Frosted Flakes and Cap'n Crunch into the cart. "David loves these," she said. But my diet books say never to eat sugar because it makes you not just fat, but *hungry,* too. The only thing all the books agree on is that you might as well kill yourself if you're hungry. The whole point of this one book was to teach you ways not to be hungry because hunger is a demon you constantly have to battle. It said that you always have to be on guard, because hunger is a tricky demon who will try to tempt you if you don't watch out.

So when Mom started rolling the cart away, I saw a cereal box that said it had a whole day's allowance of vitamins and minerals. It also had some sugar in it, but *Fun, Fit, and Fabulous* said sugar gives you energy. I've been feeling pretty tired lately, so I figured that between the sugar and the extra vitamins, I'd have enough energy to exercise. The cereal I picked was called Product 19, and the box wasn't covered with pictures of that fat Cap'n Crunch guy. So I threw it in the cart.

"What's that?" Mom asked. I thought it was pretty obvious what it was, but I pointed at the label and said, "It's Product 19, and it's healthy." "I don't think Dr. Katz wants you eating that," she said. "I don't think a doctor would want me eating Cap'n Crunch either," I answered, but that just made Mom give her nervous look to the other people buying cereal.

When we got to the next aisle, I put some wheat bread into the cart. "What's that?" Mom asked. I pointed at the wrapper and said, "It's wheat bread," but that made Mom mad. "I'm going to have to tell Dr. Katz about this," she whispered, like buying wheat bread was a federal offense. Then Mom gave me a lecture about how I'm turning out just like my Dad's crazy cousin Clara who lives in Berkeley, burns incense all the time, wears unflattering baggy dresses, and eats things like whole-grain breads and organic vegetables. It kept happening in all the aisles. Each time I'd put something healthy into the cart, Mom would shake her head and say how I'll be alone and single all my life, just like crazy cousin Clara.

After a while I got bored listening to Mom, so I started reading the ingredients on all the food labels. A major rule in *Making Friends with Food* is that you're not allowed to put any food in your mouth if you haven't read every single one of its ingredients. "If a stranger handed you something, would you put it in your mouth?" the book asks. You're supposed to say "no," obviously, because then the book says, "Uninformed eaters do that every day. That's why obesity is increasing at a dangerous rate." It's true, too. I mean, I never even noticed how fat my legs were getting.

When we finally got to the checkout line, I saw one of those collection boxes that said, PLEASE HELP THE HUNGRY. Under the sign, there was a picture of a starving girl who was probably about my age, but she had really skinny arms and legs and a fat stomach, and she was looking out at me with these huge brown eyes that took up almost her entire head, except for her lips. Her lips were turned up kind of like the Mona Lisa's. Our art teacher, Mr. Zielsky, once said that the Mona Lisa's lips were supposed to be "indicative of a secret." I remember that because I'm so bad at keeping secrets. But the secret on the girl's lips was pretty obvious: "People think I need help because I'm hungry, but *they're* the ones who need help. At least I'm thin." I could tell that's what she was thinking.

I kept staring at the girl on the poster the way Mr. Zielsky made us stare at the slide of the Mona Lisa for practically an entire period. The diet books say you'll get a fat stomach if you don't do enough sit-ups, but they forget to tell you that you'll also get a fat stomach if you diet too much. So you have to diet just enough to get the really skinny arms and legs, but not the disgusting fat stomach. That's what I'm planning on doing.

I finally stopped staring at the girl's stomach, but I couldn't stop looking at her face. I thought for a second that she was winking right at me, except I couldn't tell because then we got to the front of the line and left. The girl obviously wasn't winking, though, because then I remembered how she had those huge eyes that were opened really wide. She had the kind of big, round eyes that Mom and her friends always say are so beautiful, if you just add a little mascara to the upper lashes. I wish *I* was that beautiful.

I don't feel like talking about what happened at dinner when I didn't want to drink the milk. Basically, Mom said all I do is complain about everything, but I still wouldn't drink it. Then Dad told me I couldn't leave the table until I drank it, so I stayed at the table in the dark by myself until eleven o'clock. That's when Mom came downstairs in a pretty pink nightgown, turned on the light, started to slice off a piece of pastry from the bakery, and finally noticed me staring at her when she stood over the kitchen sink. I guess she forgot I was still downstairs. I'll bet she got caught up in some romantic movie with Robert Redford in it. Those sappy shows always end right at eleven, probably so you'll fall asleep dreaming about them.

"Go to bed," Mom said when she noticed me there. She said

it in a way that meant she was still mad at me, but I was just glad I could finally go upstairs. Then when I was leaving, Mom mumbled something like, "But the minute you wake up tomorrow, you're drinking the milk." I couldn't hear her that great because she was talking with her mouth full of pastry. It really scares me when Mom looks like that.

On the way upstairs, I started thinking about the collection box again, and I kept trying to remember if anyone put any money in. I don't think a lot of people did, even though the girl on the poster looks so hungry. You'd think people would want to help, but I guess the girl doesn't look scary enough, with those big, beautiful eyes staring right at you. If you want my opinion, they should put a picture of Mom stuffing her face over the kitchen sink on the poster instead of that beautiful African girl. *That* would scare people! I'll bet they'd get a lot more money if they did that.

# Lactose Intolerant

"Food is medicine!" Dad yelled at me yesterday morning. He's been yelling it at every meal since Dr. Katz wrote it on a prescription pad last week. But today at breakfast, Mom tried a different plan. She thought I wouldn't see sugar in our white cereal bowls, so she put some on the bottom of my bowl before I got downstairs. The idea was that I wouldn't notice and just pour my Product 19 into the bowl. But when I saw the sugar, Mom said she had no idea how it got there, and that certainly *she* didn't put it there. "How odd," she said, then she scrunched up her forehead and kept looking around for the person who put the sugar in the bowl, like we had a ghost in the kitchen. Obviously, Mom's an even worse liar than I am.

After that, Mom sat down at the table with her usual piece of toast, and we got into a big argument about milk again. I wanted to know why Mom could put nonfat milk in her coffee when I'm not allowed to drink nonfat milk. Naturally, Mom got mad at me for asking, but she also said that I can drink all the nonfat milk I want when I become a woman. But when do you become a woman? When you have your period, or go to high school, or get to vote? I wish I was a woman already so I could diet and people would think it's normal.

I never ate any breakfast because by the time we finished arguing and Mom got out a clean bowl, I was almost late for school. Right as I was walking out, Mom came to the door and shouted, "Don't forget about Dr. Katz today. I'm picking you up at 3:10, on the dot. And don't make me wait. I'm not your chauffeur, you know." I don't think anyone ever told Mom that when you have kids, you have to drive them around all day until they turn sixteen and get a driver's license. None of the ladies on her soap operas ever have to drive their kids to doctors' appointments.

Anyway, since I was going to Dr. Katz for the weight check, I figured I'd eat part of my lunch at school, just in case. I didn't know what I weighed because Dad put Mom's scale on the top shelf of his closet so I can't reach it, even with a stool. And after last week's punishment—the whole milk—who knows what Dr. Katz might make me drink if I lost more weight. Cream, maybe? So I didn't toss my lunch into my usual garbage can on the way to homeroom. Which is okay, because I never get any homework done in the library during lunch. I usually just read more diet books and make lists of foods I won't eat.

I guess it's worth it, though, because at lunch everyone at our table noticed I was losing weight and got pretty interested in how I did it. "What do you eat for breakfast?" Leslie wanted to know. "Exactly nineteen flakes of Product 19 cereal, with two ounces of nonfat milk," I said, but I made it sound like it was no big deal. "Doesn't it taste watery?" Tracy wanted to know. You can tell Tracy wouldn't last five seconds on a diet. Everyone in our group started drinking Tab instead of Coke this year, but Tracy still drinks Coke. I guess that's why she also takes her mom's diet pills sometimes. "No, it actually tastes good," I said. The truth is, it tastes pretty gross, but lately I show off when all the popular people pay attention to me like that.

Lana had questions, too. She picked up her sandwich—

turkey on wheat bread with mayonnaise and lettuce. "What about my sandwich?" she wanted to know. "Is it okay?" Lana's mom always cuts her sandwiches into neat little triangles with colored toothpicks stuck in each one, so I could see the mayonnaise seeping out. "Mayonnaise has one hundred calories per tablespoon," I said, then I shook my head so she'd know you can't ever eat that. That's when Lana put her sandwich away and took out an apple instead.

Then everyone started crowding around me and asking questions all at once, like I was a movie star or something. They wanted me to look in their lunch bags and tell them how to stay thin or get even thinner, like I was doing. I know this sounds conceited to say, but by the end of the lunch period, I was almost as popular as I used to be back in first grade when I still had blondish hair. Which is why I never ate my own lunch. I mean, if I ate a bologna sandwich with mayonnaise on Wonder bread, everyone would definitely think I was a phony. So I only ate a banana. Lately I started putting something healthy like an apple or a banana in my lunch before I leave for school, even though it always makes Mom ask, "What's that?"

I guess if I actually ate my sandwich at lunch, I would have weighed more when Dr. Katz put me on the scale after school. I lost three pounds, though, which didn't make Dr. Katz happy. Right away he wanted to see us in his office to discuss my situation again. He loves calling my diet a "situation." So we sat down on the two chairs in his office, and Dr. Katz sat behind his huge wooden desk. Behind the desk there was a big shelf crammed with books that all had tongue depressors sticking out of them as bookmarks. I tried reading the titles of the books, but Dr. Katz started talking.

"I'm awfully confused," Dr. Katz said. "You say that you're eating, but your mother here says that you aren't eating, and then, of course, the scale says that you're sixty pounds. How do you explain all of this?" Dr. Katz was squinting at me like it was really bright in his office and he might need sunglasses.

"I don't know how to explain it," I said. "Maybe something's wrong with your scale." I figured something must be wrong with his scale, since my legs still looked fat, uncrossed. "Oh, please," Mom butted in, but since she never has anything to say after that, everyone was quiet again.

Dr. Katz was looking right at me and his eyes squinted so much I thought they might close all the way. "I gave you instructions, darlin'—a prescription, if you will—to drink three eight-ounce glasses of whole milk per day. Your mother here says that you haven't been drinking them." He was really stuck on those three eight-ounce glasses of whole milk.

"Whole milk makes me sick," I told him. "I can't digest it." It was a lie, but at lunch in the library yesterday, I read about people who can't digest milk. It gives them cramps.

That's when Mom butted in again. "She drank whole milk as a baby and had no problem digesting it." It's true, too. Mom didn't breast-feed me or anything, probably because it would ruin her lunch dates. Whenever she sees mothers breast-feeding their babies in restaurants, she always tells the waiter to make them stop. "Well, it makes me sick now," I answered, even though for once Mom sounded more logical than me.

The funny thing is, Dr. Katz believed me. "Sometimes people become lactose intolerant as they enter puberty," he told Mom. I started saying "lactose intolerant" over and over in my head so I'd remember it. Mom never remembers anything, and I knew Dad would ask about it later. "The thing is, darlin', if whole milk doesn't agree with you, we need to find something else with an equivalent number of calories that does." I wanted to tell Dr. Katz that nothing with the equivalent number of calories will ever agree with me, because I'll never agree to be fat. But I knew Dr. Katz wouldn't understand, so I kept on lying, even though I didn't want to.

I told Dr. Katz that *I am* eating enough calories, even without the whole milk. Then I went into my backpack and ripped out the page from my notebook that had a chart I made in French class today. My book *The New You* said to make a chart called "The Old You." In one column you have to write down all the foods you used to eat, and in the other column you have to write the number of calories in each food. It's supposed to show you what a pig "The Old You" was, because "The New You" would never eat like that. But I told Dr. Katz that I eat everything on my list. That's when Mom yelled, "See, she's reading diet books now!" I asked Mom why I can't read diet books if she reads about diets in *Redbook* and *Vogue* and *McCall's* all the time, but she just looked at Dr. Katz, like *he* was supposed answer my question.

Dr. Katz didn't have much to say about the diet books, though. Instead he kept reading my food chart and clicking these two tongue depressors against his desk like he was a drummer in a rock band. Finally he stopped and said, "If you're really eating everything on this list, then you wouldn't be losing weight." He was looking me right in the eye again, and I looked right back in his. I was trying to think of something to say.

"I think something's wrong with my metabolism," I blurted out. I know about metabolism because ever since I was a kid, Mom would always talk about how lucky I am that I can eat a lot and not gain weight, just like Dad. "Lori got her father's metabolism and my good looks," she always told people when they said how pretty I was. Then she'd say how lucky it was that David was the one who got her metabolism, being a boy and all. She didn't want her daughter to be "cursed" with slow metabolism. Like girls with slow metabolism are witches.

Anyway, I was hoping Dr. Katz might decide to leave me alone for once, but then the worst thing happened. He told Mom that I have to go to Children's Hospital and have what's called a GI test, so he can make sure that everything's okay with my digestion. He explained how I'll have to drink a pink fluid, then the doctors will take pictures of it as it goes through my digestive system. He said he'll make all the arrangements, and it will only take a few hours on an outpatient basis. I knew that meant I'd have to miss school, which made me nervous because I might miss a test. Mom got nervous, too. "Will I need to wait with her, or can I drop her off and pick her up when it's over?" she asked Dr. Katz. Like I said, Mom hates being a chauffeur.

When we were driving home, Mom was singing along with her favorite sappy radio station about love and romance and stuff. Mom has a pretty good voice, but it bugs me because she always sings like *she's* the lady they wrote the song about. I was in charge of holding on to the hospital orders since Mom always loses things, like valet parking tickets and shopping receipts, which makes Dad mad. I wanted to ask Mom when she was planning on taking me to have the test done so I could tell my teachers in advance, but when I looked over at her, I noticed she had tears in her eyes. Mom gets very dramatic when she sings that part in the song "Evergreen" that goes, "Love, soft as an easy chair . . . love . . . fresh as the morning air." It's like she's remembering some incredibly romantic moment with a long-lost lover. She was singing that part so loud she probably wouldn't have heard my question anyway.

So I looked over the slips of paper to see if maybe a date was already scheduled for the test, but Dr. Katz has terrible writing, and I couldn't read most of what he wrote. There was nothing marked under "appointment time," but there was something scribbled across the top of each page. It was right under my name in huge red letters, with a box around it, but it was too messy to read. I kept squinting at the letters anyway, though, and finally I figured out what they said: LACTOSE INTOLERANT. Thank God there won't be any whole milk in the pink fluid they'll make me drink.

# If You Can Pinch an Inch

Dad was already home when we got back from Dr. Katz's office. The stock market closes early in Los Angeles, so Dad's always sitting in his study and smoking his pipe by five o'clock. Mom told Dad how I lost three pounds, and when Mom started screaming, Dad shut the door. I stood outside and tried to listen anyway, but Dad had the TV on and some man was yelling out a bunch of stock prices. I could only hear words like "crazy," "diet," "lying," and "hospital" in between all the numbers. Whatever Mom and Dad said in there, though, I think they decided to stop bugging me until after the hospital test. I mean, Mom didn't even ask "What's that?" when I said I wanted to buy Special K cereal.

The reason I wanted to buy Special K is because I saw a commercial for it on TV. In the commercial, there's a lady in a white bathing suit who keeps smiling and walking around a big swimming pool, just so you can see how thin she is. But then she comes up really close and looks you right in the eye and asks, "Can you pinch an inch?" She means on your stomach. She's still smiling, of course, because when *she* pinches her own stomach there's no fat at all. She's pretty happy about that. "If you can pinch an inch," she says, "then you need Special K cereal."

Even though the lady bugged me, I still tried her pinching test after the commercial ended. If I pinch above my belly button, I can't pinch an inch, but if I do it underneath, I can almost pinch an inch. So now I eat Special K instead of Product 19.

The other thing I'll eat for breakfast, because you don't have to worry about people contaminating it with whole milk or sugar, is a piece of wheat toast with three glasses of water. "Drink eight tall glasses of water every day," *Thirty Days to Thin* said. "You'll be surprised how full you'll feel." I never feel full from the water, but I still make sure to drink eight tall glasses each day, just in case. Except we're not allowed to bring any drinks into the classroom, so I'm always asking permission to get a drink of water at school. I ask so much that Mr. Darlington started letting me keep the hall pass in my desk so I don't disrupt the class every five minutes. Now I just get up and run to the water fountain whenever I feel like it, but I can tell it bugs him.

That's why Mr. Darlington handed me a pink slip during history today. It said I was supposed to go down to the guidance counselor that period. When I went to Miss Shaw's office, I figured I'd see the usual IQ test stuff laid out on the table, but there weren't any puzzles, and Miss Shaw told me in a really friendly voice to come in and sit down. I knew something was up.

Miss Shaw doesn't have a nice office like Dr. Katz does. She has an ugly metal desk with stacks of paper all over it and drawers that don't even close all the way. The school gave her one of those high-backed orange plastic chairs that has a tear right over where her left shoulder is when she's sitting in it. She also used to have a picture of her and some guy on a shelf behind the desk, but last time I was in her office, the picture wasn't there anymore. Neither was the diamond ring she used to wear.

I sat down and asked Miss Shaw where the puzzles were. "We're not doing any testing today," she said. She kept smiling at me really wide, so I could see her teeth and everything. She had a piece of something stuck between two of them, and I wondered if maybe it was part of the muffin—225 calories— that was sitting on her desk. She's very skinny and I couldn't imagine her ever eating that muffin, but I didn't say anything. Miss Shaw was quiet, too. She just kept grinning, like she was about to tell me something terrible. I figured she'd say that they decided I have to go to high school early because of my IQ, even though I don't want to.

"I just want to see how you're doing," Miss Shaw said instead. I thought that was kind of weird, especially since they took me out of history class for this, but I told Miss Shaw I was doing fine. I really wanted to know what was going on. Then Miss Shaw leaned forward across her desk like she was about to tell me a secret and whispered, "I thought we might have a little chat this morning." A chat. Like I would really be friends with someone in her twenties. "You want to have a chat?" I asked Miss Shaw. "Yes," she said again, "I thought we might have a little chat, talk about what's been going on."

The thing is, I was missing the Pilgrims film in history, and I was getting really worried because we're having a big test on it next week. I had to get back to class, or I might not get an A. So I know this was a mean thing to do, but all of a sudden I said, "Okay, I'll chat. Let's chat about your boyfriend. Does he have a new girlfriend yet?" This time I smiled, but only for a second because Miss Shaw's face turned kind of white. Then I felt terrible, but it was too late to take it back, even though I really wanted to. I thought I also saw Miss Shaw's eyes get a little teary, but she was looking down at her desk, so I couldn't tell for sure.

That's when she finally got to the point. "Look, Lori, the truth is, we're all a bit concerned about you. Mr. Miller said that you go to the library alone at lunch every day. Mrs. Jacobs said that you demanded an A-plus on your report card, when we don't give pluses on report cards, even if you do extra credit. Miss Drabin said that you made a disrespectful comment about her tennis skirt being too short. Mrs. Rivers said that you insist on making up your own homework assignments, and Mr. Darlington said that you leave class to get a drink of water every few minutes."

Miss Shaw waited a long time for me to say something, but when I didn't, she started talking again. I could tell this would be the bad part, the part where they'd make me go to high school early. I mean, she just got through explaining why every single teacher wanted to get *rid* of me. But instead Miss Shaw started saying something about how I'm losing weight, and how I should tell her if I have a medical problem. I wasn't paying that much attention because I kept wondering why her boyfriend dumped her even though she's so skinny.

"Are you listening to me?" Miss Shaw asked. "I'm trying to talk to you about your situation." Everyone calls my diet a "situation." Miss Shaw told me that she wanted to talk to me first, but if I didn't feel comfortable discussing my situation, she would have to call my parents. So *that* was the bad news. It was a hundred times worse than I expected. I'd die if Miss Shaw called my parents, so I told her she was right about me having a medical problem. I said that I'm lactose intolerant, and that I have to get a GI test. Then, just to make sure she'd leave me alone, I said I'd have to miss half a day of school to take the test at a hospital. The hospital made it sound really serious. "Please don't call my parents," I begged. "They're already worried about my situation." I called it a situation to kiss up to Miss Shaw.

I felt bad about lying to Miss Shaw, because then she got up and hugged me and said she knew I'd be okay and I shouldn't be afraid of going to a hospital for a test. She's pretty nice, I guess. It's weird, but when she hugged me, I almost told her that things aren't okay. I wanted to tell her how my parents won't let me eat what I want, my friends only care about what they wear, no one's interested in the things I like anymore, my teachers keep giving me bad grades for making the assignments more interesting, everyone thinks I'm abnormal, no matter what I do, and nothing's fair, like how she got dumped by her boyfriend even though she's so skinny.

I almost started telling her these things, but she was still hugging me and all of a sudden I felt her stomach pressed up against my ribs. So when Miss Shaw finally let go, I looked down at her belly and saw that *she* could probably pinch an inch, too. I didn't notice that when she was sitting behind her desk. "Let me know how the hospital test goes," she said, but I wanted to tell her to buy Special K so she could find a new boyfriend. Then I decided not to say anything, because lately every time I say something, someone calls me crazy.

Before I left her office, Miss Shaw wrote me a yellow absence slip for tomorrow morning. I thanked her about fifty times and ran back to history class because there were still ten minutes left in the period. But out in the hallway, I stopped for a second to read the yellow slip. Under "Time Out" it said, "Through lunch period." I was happy I'd get to miss lunch. Then, under "Reason for Absence" it said, "Medical situation."


It was pretty dark in the history classroom because the Pilgrims film was still going, but I could kind of see Mr. Darlington sitting behind his desk doing a crossword puzzle. He was chewing on his pencil, and he tried to hide the crossword when I got close, because teachers are supposed to act interested in all the boring movies they show us. Everyone looked at me when I handed him the yellow slip, but Mr. Darlington told the class to turn around and watch the rest of the film. Then I went to my desk to take notes. It was a two-part movie, and the first part ended where all the people on the boat were starving. You were supposed to be scared they might die, even though everyone knows they make it to America and get fat from eating too much turkey, especially the dark meat. But I won't get to see that part, because of the hospital tomorrow.

# Level F, Section Pink

The car ride over to Children's Hospital was like every other car ride with Mom. She was listening to her favorite radio station and belting out "Close to You" along with Karen Carpenter when all of a sudden she slammed on the brakes and yelled, "Shit!" That usually means we're lost. Children's Hospital is somewhere near Hollywood, but Mom always gets lost when we go too far from Beverly Hills.

I reached into the glove compartment to try to find a map, but Mom grabbed it from me and held it upside down. Last night Dad wrote out directions for her, and today Mom kept reading them over and over to the map, like it would talk back and tell us how to get there. The thing is, Mom was trying to drive again the whole time she was looking at the upside-down map and the directions, and we must have broken some law because a policeman pulled up next to us on his motorcycle. He didn't give us a ticket, though, probably because Mom started crying and kept talking about rushing her daughter to the hospital. Like I was dying from a diet. Then the policeman turned on his siren and told us to follow him all the way to Outpatient Admitting. You could tell Mom got a big kick out of getting the royal treatment. She wasn't crying anymore when we got there.


Because of the policeman, we were early for my appointment. I didn't feel like watching the cartoons on the TV in the waiting area, so I took my Thomas Jefferson report out of my backpack and checked it over. Yesterday Mr. Darlington said I could do an extra credit report if that would make me feel better about missing the second part of the Pilgrims film. Then I wanted to make next week's diet lists for Leslie and Lana, but I obviously couldn't do that with Mom sitting right next to me. So I was getting bored, and then my stomach started making noises because I wasn't allowed to eat or drink anything for twelve hours before the test. Not that I would have anyway. But Mom said I sounded hungry and that we could go out to lunch before she took me back to school. Mom thinks going to lunch is incredibly exciting, so I guess she was trying to be nice. But I think she forgot why we were at the hospital in the first place. I mean, I already decided not to eat anything the whole day to make up for the calories in the pink fluid.

Finally a big, friendly nurse with white hair called me in. I said I thought it was funny that she looked like Santa Claus, without the beard, but Mom started tearing up again. I felt bad because there wasn't anyone out in the waiting room to hold her hand the way I do in Dr. Katz's office. So I told Mom I'd be fine and not to worry, but she still reached into her purse and pulled out some tissues to wipe her eyes. Then Mrs. Claus made me go in, but I asked if she'd bring my mom some *Redbook* magazines so she could read about diets and makeup and stuff while I took the test, and Mrs. Claus said she would.

I didn't go right into the testing room, though. First Mrs. Claus took me to this tiny room with a sink in it and handed me the pink fluid. It looked like a strawberry milk shake, but I knew it didn't have any milk because I already gave them those slips that said "lactose intolerant" on the top. Then I tried really hard to stop thinking about the diet book that said not to put things from strangers in your mouth, but I still couldn't drink the shake. "Don't worry, it doesn't taste bad," Mrs. Claus said. "I sweetened it up for you so it'll taste like candy."

She was obviously trying to poison me, so I put the cup on the edge of the sink and told Mrs. Claus I didn't want a shake full of sugar. I wanted just the stuff they needed for the test to work, even if it tasted gross. But she told me not to worry since she didn't put any sugar in the shake in case I have diabetes. She said she used another sweetener so it was safe to drink. I didn't know what she meant by safe, but if the shake was *really* safe, it wouldn't have any calories. So I asked to see the ingredients, but everyone started paging Mrs. Claus on the speakers and you could tell she just wanted me to drink it. I kept asking anyway, though.

"Look, honey, I don't have time to go find the ingredients for you," she said, "and you need to drink this right away because the doctors are waiting in the testing room." When she called me honey, that got me thinking that maybe she sweetened the shake with honey—65 calories per tablespoon. Then Mrs. Claus gave me the cup again, but I just held it in my hands. "We've given this same shake to thousands of kids just like you, and no one's ever gotten sick from it," she said. I didn't care if I got *sick* from it, I just didn't want to get *fat* from it. But then I remembered how I didn't eat breakfast and I wasn't planning on eating lunch, so I closed my eyes and poured the pink fluid down my throat. I have to admit, it tasted pretty good.

After that, Mrs. Claus took me to a dressing room to change into one of those hospital gowns like you see on TV. I tried to leave it kind of baggy so the doctors couldn't see how fat I looked after drinking the pink fluid. Luckily, the testing room was dark, except for lots of screens that lit up the room. All I did was lie down and watch the doctors take pictures of the pink fluid moving through my body. I'm not bragging or anything, but I looked great in the pictures. My stomach looked really tiny, kind of like a grape. Which didn't make much sense, since I can almost pinch an inch. So I tried looking at my stomach under the gown, but the doctors told me not to move. They said I could watch everything on the screen if I wanted, but I had to stay still the whole time. Then I asked them to let me know when the shake was being changed into fat, because I wanted to watch that part carefully, but they just laughed and never told me when it happened.

That was the whole test. When I got out into the waiting room, Mom was watching a soap opera they had on the TV. I walked over and sat down next to her, but she wasn't crying anymore. She just pointed at some actor on the screen and said, "Now *he's* handsome, Lori. What do you think of him?" like she was planning on fixing me up on a date when I'm twenty. I said he was okay, but Mom wouldn't stop talking about how gorgeous he was. I finally agreed with her just so we could change the subject. Then Mom started getting her stuff together and I noticed that Mrs. Claus never brought the *Redbook*s like she promised. I wondered what Mom did before the soap operas came on, and I got kind of scared for her. But there weren't any tissues lying around, so I figured she was okay.

It took Mom forever to pack up her big purse, so I was waiting when I saw a girl about my age sitting across the room with her mom. They were laughing about something they both thought was hilarious. I was looking at the girl's painted fingernails and her nice clothes and her skinny legs, and thinking about how she looked a little like Donna Landers. She had big blue eyes and a purple baseball cap, the kind they have at Fred Segal's. Then she noticed me looking at her, except she didn't pretend to fall asleep like Donna would have. She even smiled at me, but I was embarrassed for staring and didn't smile back. I just looked down and saw the girl and her mom holding hands. But the girl said hi, so I had to look up again. That's when I noticed how the girl didn't have any hair under her baseball cap. Her hair wasn't tucked under in a ponytail like I thought when I saw her at first. I swear, she was even balder than Dad!

Mom's purse was finally packed and we were ready to leave, so I got up and said bye, and the girl said bye back. Our moms smiled at each other, then her mom told my mom how the weight loss stops after treatment, and how Children's Hospital has a great program, so my mom should know I was in good hands. Mom sure stopped smiling after that. "Thank you," she said, but not nice or anything. More like the way she says thank you to waiters who take too long bringing her iced tea. Then she grabbed my hand and practically pulled me out the door.

Mom didn't say anything on the way to the parking lot, and when we got there we couldn't find the car. Dad's always telling Mom to write down the level we're parked on but she never does, probably because the tissues in her purse take up too much room for any paper. But I remembered that we were parked on level F, section pink, for "Pink Fluid." It was 12:30 when we got in the car, halfway through lunchtime at school, so Mom said that we'd pick up a sandwich on the way back.

I told Mom I was full from the pink fluid, but then she got mad at me. Partly for being full, but mostly because I look so embarrassing that she can't even take me to a hospital without people thinking I have some disease. She was yelling so loud that she didn't even whisper the words "hospital" or "cancer" like she usually does. She was getting pretty dramatic, maybe because she just watched all those soap operas in the waiting room. I tried explaining that *of course* the lady thought I was sick—only sick people take tests at hospitals. It obviously had nothing to do with the way I look. But Mom said she was buying me a sandwich whether I ate it or not, and when the tests come back and Dr. Katz finds out that nothing's wrong with me, I'll be very sorry, Lori Ellen. Believe me, I already was.

# Facts and Figure

Last night I was in my room making new diet lists for me and my bird, Chrissy, when Dad knocked on my door. So I stuffed *My Calorie-Counting Companion* and birdseed ingredients into my desk and told Dad to come in. He said he wanted to talk to me. Then he moved my floppy Raggedy Ann doll out of the way, sat down on my bed, and took a deep breath. I knew bad news was coming.

"Your mother and I are very concerned about you," Dad said. Which really meant that Mom was getting nervous because of my diet, and if Mom gets nervous, she drives Dad crazy until they get into a big argument about it. Then Mom makes Dad try to talk some sense into me, and Dad comes in and says how concerned he is. So all of sudden he asked me a bunch of questions in a row, like: Why won't I eat? Why do I think I'm fat? Why have I become so "downbeat"? Why can't I listen to Dr. Katz? Why can't I just be happy?

I told Dad that I won't eat because I don't *think* I'm fat, I *know* I'm fat. I said I'm downbeat because I hate being fat. I said I don't listen to Dr. Katz because a fat person's a pretty bad judge of whether someone else is fat. And I said I can't just be happy until I'm thin. But Dad didn't think my answers were logical enough.

It turns out that Dad did some research, and this is what he found out: A girl my age needs 2000 calories per day to grow. (But I don't want to grow, I want to shrink.) Because I have high metabolism, I need 2500 calories per day to grow. (No, my high metabolism just means I don't have to do as many sets of leg-lifts in the dark after everyone's asleep.) When you develop, fat is distributed unevenly, but after you go through "changes" (Dad's face turned kind of red and he couldn't even say the word "puberty"), the fat will go back to normal. (Fat never goes back to normal, it just gives you cottage-cheese thighs. It's true. I read it in Mom's *Redbook*.)

Then Dad said that if I don't believe him, Dr. Katz has charts of things like height and weight and average waist sizes for girls my age. He said when I go back to the doctor, Dr. Katz will show me the facts and the figures, and then I'll realize how ridiculous I'm being. "I don't care about the facts, I only care about the figures—my figure, and that it's thin," I said, but Dad didn't smile or anything. He just kept smoothing out the red hair on my Raggedy Ann doll. I'm telling you, no one has a sense of humor anymore.

Finally Dad said that we'll wait for the results of the hospital test, and then we can decide on a plan from there. I wanted to tell Dad that I already had a plan—I had meals planned for the next month, I even had lists of things I didn't plan on eating for the rest of my life—but I figured he'd never understand. So I thanked Dad for trying to talk to me, then I told him to tell Mom I was sorry for making her so nervous all the time. I wasn't just saying it, either. I feel terrible for making everyone nervous, even Chrissy. I've been scaring her at night when I run laps around my room, so last night I put a sheet over her cage, but I don't think it helped.

All day at school I couldn't stop worrying about my appointment with Dr. Katz and about what he'd say when he got the test results back. Most of the teachers have been pretty nice lately, I guess because Miss Shaw told them how I had to miss school because of my "medical situation." Except for Miss Drabin, who wouldn't let me go to the boys' PE class because she said it would be too strenuous. But I didn't care that much, because today the girls' class was doing testing for the Presidential Physical Fitness Award. I'm in really good shape from all the sit-ups and leg-lifts and laps around my room I do at night, so I did sixty sit-ups in one minute, ran seven laps in twelve minutes, and did ten pull-ups, which meant I won the award. Everyone was cheering for me and saying how great I did, but then Leslie got jealous that I set all the records, because she used to be the best athlete in our grade. She even told Miss Drabin that it was easier for me to do all those pull-ups because I have no boobs to lift up. Then Lana started making fun of me, too, and everyone stopped cheering.

That's when Miss Drabin told Leslie and Lana that a medical situation is nothing to make fun of, but Leslie told her that I was a liar and I was just on a diet. "You're both on a diet, too! You're on *my* diet!" I yelled, but no one heard me because the boys' basketball came flying over to where our class was standing and everyone ran after it. Then Miss Drabin smiled at Mr. Brodsky and said we could go to the locker room early and change. I would have used the extra time to sneak into Miss Drabin's office and weigh myself, but Leslie and Lana were hogging the scale and I didn't want to be late for science. I'm not making diet lists for Leslie and Lana ever again. I'm serious.

When I finally got to Dr. Katz's office after school, he didn't say anything about the hospital test. He just kept asking a bunch of questions like how school was and how my friends were. I told him school was fine and my friends were okay, which was obviously a lie, but I wasn't in the mood to have an entire conversation. I really wanted Dr. Katz to weigh me already and get it over with. My plan was that if I gained weight, I'd drink only liquids for two days, then I'd eat 500 calories per day for two days for energy, then I'd eat 400 a day until I get thin. But if I lost weight, I'd just eat 400 calories a day until I get thin.

Dr. Katz didn't seem to be in much of a hurry to weigh me, though. He just kept asking me more questions. First he wanted to know why I'm losing weight if everything is fine. I told him that he didn't even weigh me yet so he couldn't *know* I'm losing weight, but Dr. Katz said he had "a strong feeling" that I would weigh less than I did last week. He also said he had "a strong feeling" that I lost more than a pound since last week. Then, like he was a psychic or something, he said he had "a strong feeling" that things weren't fine at school, and his "instincts" told him things would only get worse if I didn't talk about them. I thought he might ask to read my palm next, but instead he finally told me to take off my shoes and step onto the scale.

Dr. Katz's psychic prediction that I lost more than a pound this week made me feel kind of thin. So when I stepped onto the scale, I pretended to be that actress in *A Chorus Line* stepping onto the stage. I had great boobs and a great butt and I was light enough to fly. I watched Dr. Katz move the metal weight to the left, and when the scale still didn't balance, he squinted and moved it even more to the left. Then his forehead wrinkled up, and he told me to put on my shoes and go to his office so we could talk.

Dr. Katz went into the waiting room and whispered something to Mom, then I met him in his office. He told me that the GI test was normal, that my mom says I'm still not eating anything, that the school called her because they think I'm acting even more different than I normally do, and that I lost two pounds in a week and none of it's water weight.

That's when Dr. Katz grabbed two tongue depressors from his coat and started banging them together. For a long time, he kept trying to get me to talk about school and friends and boys and puberty, and when I said that all those things were incredibly boring compared to things like chess strategies and life as a woman during Thomas Jefferson's time, Dr. Katz told me he was making me go to a psychiatrist. "You mean you're sending me to a shrink?" I asked. I couldn't believe Dr. Katz thought I was crazy. "Well darlin', some people call psychiatrists shrinks," he said, "but I think you need to talk to someone about your situation." "What situation?" I asked, but Dr. Katz didn't answer, naturally. He just pushed a button on his phone and told his nurse to have Mom join us.

When Mom came in, Dr. Katz told her that I have to go see a psychiatrist named Sol Gold. Dr. Katz said he's known Dr. Gold for many years and that Dr. Gold can help me with my situation. "WHAT SITUATION?" I asked again, but Dr. Katz just kept talking about how great Dr. Gold is. I kind of wondered how Dr. Katz knew that Dr. Gold was so good, but then I figured he probably goes to Dr. Gold for his own weight problem, too. Obviously, it's not helping.

Then Mom started telling Dr. Katz how convenient it is that I can walk to Dr. Gold's office after school. It's on "couch row" in Beverly Hills, which is only a few blocks from our house, but I told Dr. Katz that I don't have time to go to Dr. Gold because I have typing on Wednesdays, Mentally Gifted Minors literature on Tuesdays and Thursdays, science enrichment on Fridays, and I just started piano on Mondays. I'm too busy. That's when Dr. Katz started pulling out the facts and figures, just like Dad said he would.

Dr. Katz took some books from his shelf and turned to the pages with the tongue depressors sticking out. Then he showed me how according to the charts I'm in the bottom tenth percentile in weight for my height, and the bottom fortieth percentile in height for my age, and that if I don't eat, soon I won't be on the charts at all. I kind of thought that would be neat, so I asked if I could take a height-weight chart home with me instead of a helium balloon, but Dr. Katz didn't give me the chart or the balloon. He just blew out a bunch of air that smelled like corned beef, and I held my breath in case any calories went up my nose.

After that, Mom thanked Dr. Katz for the psychiatrist's name and told him that the shrink would surely be good for me because she always knew I was different. Her biggest complaint to Dr. Katz was that all the other girls at school are going shopping alone for the first time and talking about boys, but all I do is add up numbers of calories all day. She thought maybe the problem has to do with me being too involved with my math class, and maybe if I get taken out of advanced math and put back in regular math, then I won't be so interested in adding up numbers.

But Dr. Katz told Mom that before she takes me out of advanced math, she should read a book from his shelf called *The Golden Cage*. It looked brand new. I figured it might have more facts and figures in it, but Dr. Katz didn't open up the book and show me any charts this time. He just started talking to Mom again like I wasn't even in the room. It really bugs me when people do that, even though I always listen anyway.

Dr. Katz told Mom that I have a disease called anorexia nervosa. When I heard the word "nervosa," I thought maybe Mom had the disease, too, because she's always so nervous. But Dr. Katz said it's Latin and it means I get nervous about gaining weight. Then he held up *The Golden Cage* and wrote the book's name on a prescription pad for Mom. He told her to read the book carefully because it would help her understand my situation, and to have Dad read it, too. "WHAT SITUATION?!" I asked for the millionth time, but Dr. Katz just told Mom to call Dr. Gold for me, and also to make an appointment for next Friday's weight check.

# Shrink Me

Today was my first appointment with Dr. Gold, and of course Mom was more nervous about my appointment than me. She went through my closet before school and started picking out different outfits that looked cute, like we were deciding what I should wear to a boy-girl party. She even made me change sweaters three times, and I ended up wearing an itchy mohair one. "I can't believe you're dressing me up for the shrink!" I said, but Mom told me I wasn't dressed up. Then the second I met Julie on the corner to walk to school, she asked what I was all dressed up for. I said I wasn't all dressed up, but Julie said I normally don't wear mohair sweaters and lip gloss unless I like someone. She kept bugging me the whole way because she thought I wouldn't tell her who I liked.

I finally got rid of Julie at school, but then I was walking over to my usual trash can to throw out my lunch when Jason Meyer cornered me in the hallway. Jason always tries to hang out with the popular boys, but believe me, they hate his guts because he makes stupid jokes all the time. Anyway, since I haven't been talking to Leslie or anyone since they made a big deal about the Presidential Physical Fitness Award, I didn't even know about the school carnival this Friday. So when Jason asked me to go with him, I was pretty surprised. I mean, I wasn't planning on going in the first place, but even if I was, I'd never go with Jason, even if I'm not popular anymore.

The problem is, I wanted to be nice about it because everyone else is so mean to Jason, but I also didn't want Leslie or Lana to see me in the hall with him. So I told Jason it had nothing to do with him personally, it's just that I didn't want to go to the carnival. It was a big lie, of course, because if Chris asked me, I'd probably go with him, but I figured Jason would fall for it because he's so dense. But he's so dense that he wouldn't leave me alone about going with him, even though I only made up the lie in the first place so I wouldn't hurt his feelings. Then the bell rang and I had to run all the way to homeroom so Mr. Miller wouldn't give me a tardy. The worst part was, I never got a chance to dump my lunch. That meant I had to smell food in my desk until recess, which made me kind of hungry.

When it was finally time for my appointment after school, the mohair sweater Mom made me wear was itching like mad. Mom decided to drive me there because she said she didn't want Dr. Gold to think I was an orphan. She sure seemed to be worrying a lot about what Dr. Gold might think of her, even though *I* was the one who was supposed to be crazy. Dr. Gold didn't have any *Redbook* magazines in his waiting room, though, so Mom decided to prepare me for my appointment while we waited. "Try to remember what he says when he explains why you're doing this to us," she said. "Don't forget to tell him that we can't take much more of this, and that we just don't know what to do with you anymore."

Finally Dr. Gold came out and shook Mom's hand, and told me to go inside. Mom smiled and started to say how concerned she was about me, but right when Dr. Gold was about to close the door, she started crying. I told Dr. Gold that maybe Mom should take the appointment instead of me, but Dr. Gold just said it was my session and he didn't want to take up my time. Then he talked to Mom until she calmed down and left. I wish he'd show me how to do that sometime. I figured Dr. Katz was right about Dr. Gold being so great, but when Dr. Gold came in and sat down on his big leather chair, I knew he couldn't help me. You should see him. He's almost as fat as Dr. Katz.

"Why don't you tell me a little bit about what's been going on recently," Dr. Gold said in a really quiet voice. I figured Dr. Katz forgot to tell me that you're supposed to whisper at the shrink, so I whispered to Dr. Gold that I knew Dr. Katz already told him about me, and it was stupid for me to repeat everything. But Dr. Gold whispered that he wanted to hear in my own words what's been going on, and I have to admit, I kind of liked him for asking. No one cares what I think anymore. Then I whispered to Dr. Gold that the only thing going on is that everyone's making a big deal because I'm on a diet, and that I don't understand why I have to see a psychiatrist when everyone who's popular at school is on a diet, too.

That made Dr. Gold nod at me for a long time. I didn't know why he bothered asking me a question if he wasn't planning on talking anymore. He was really boring me, so I looked down at my thighs and tried to multiply eight sets of leg-lifts per leg, times 40 calories, times seven days, and divide that by 3500 calories, which equals a pound, all in my head. I was right in the middle of multiplying when Dr. Gold asked if I thought the girls at school who diet are overweight. It was such a stupid question that I forgot to whisper when I answered. "*Of course* they aren't overweight, didn't I already say they were *popular*?" I mean, duh. But Dr. Gold just nodded again, then he wanted to know if I thought I was overweight. I pointed at my uncrossed thighs so he could see for himself, and he nodded like crazy. Finally, someone understands.

After that, Dr. Gold got out some paper and a pencil and asked me to draw pictures of my friends and me. I told him I'm bad at art, but he just held out the pencil and smiled. I was starting to think that maybe something was wrong with Dr. Gold—you know, nodding and smiling all the time for no reason. He kind of scared me, so I figured I should draw what he wanted. I took the pencil and drew Leslie, Lana, Tracy, and me. Except I'm the one with the thunder thighs in the picture, not Tracy. Then I gave the drawing back to Dr. Gold.

Dr. Gold looked at the drawing and nodded some more, then he gave me more paper and asked me to draw my "ideal" of what I want to look like. He was still whispering the whole time. I almost complained, but when I saw Dr. Gold smiling at me again, I decided to do what he asked. He was really giving me the creeps.

So I picked up the pencil and drew a girl I want to look like. She was tall and skinny, but she had my face and hair. When Dr. Gold took the drawing back, he didn't nod. "This is a stick figure," he said, like I didn't understand the assignment the first time. "Try to draw a *realistic* picture of how you'd like to look. Don't worry if you aren't very good at art." He must have thought I was terrible at art. I tried explaining how that was *exactly* the way I want to look, but Dr. Gold said I wouldn't be alive if I looked like that drawing. "Well if you don't like it, then stop asking me to draw pictures of what I want to look like," I said, then I told him to forget the whole thing. What an idiot.

But Dr. Gold didn't seem like he was forgetting the whole thing, because he kept looking at my drawings and nodding to himself. Finally he asked about my family. "Tell me about what's been going on during dinnertime in your house," he said. I was wondering how much time was left before I could go home and exercise, but I didn't want Dr. Gold to tell Dr. Katz that I'm crazy, so I decided to answer him. "Well, you know, we eat around 6:30. Maria and Mom make dinner, and Dad tells jokes, and David and I laugh and talk about how fun school was," I said. Except I was really talking about the family on *The Brady Bunch*. The truth is, I didn't feel like telling Dr. Gold anything personal anymore.

After that, Dr. Gold wanted to know what I like to do for fun. I have to admit, I was pretty surprised since that's not one of the usual questions adults keep asking me lately. So I told him that I like to play chess and read books and do math problems, but the minute I said it, I wanted to take it back. I figured Dr. Gold would definitely tell Dr. Katz I'm crazy because I didn't say that I like to go shopping and follow boys around all day.

But Dr. Gold didn't call me crazy. Instead he took a chessboard out of his desk and started setting up the pieces. He even said I could be white if I wanted, since white goes first, and we played chess until it was time to go. I was three moves away from winning when his light went on, which Dr. Gold said meant that someone else came in the entrance door and was waiting for the next appointment. Probably some other lady on a diet.

On the way out, I asked Dr. Gold if he thought I was crazy. I really wanted to know. He said that no one thinks I'm crazy, but I told him that my parents think I'm crazy, and so do my teachers and friends and Dr. Katz. Then he didn't say anything, so I asked him why I have to go to a shrink if I'm not crazy. That's when Dr. Gold said that people see psychiatrists just to have someone to talk to. I'll bet Dr. Katz told him how I have no friends left at school. I knew Dr. Gold wanted me to go because he had another person waiting, but I had one last question first.

"Why are psychiatrists called shrinks?" I asked. Dr. Gold laughed for the first time and said that the word comes from an old wives' tale about healers who had the power to shrink the heads of their patients. Then he practically pushed me out the exit door. So I walked to the elevator, then I figured I'd take the stairs for the exercise. I usually count the number of stairs to figure out how many calories I'm burning, but today I was still thinking about what Dr. Gold said. I mean, if a shrink can shrink you, maybe seeing Dr. Gold once a week won't be that bad.

When I got home from Dr. Gold's, Mom and Dad wanted to know how the appointment went. "What did Dr. Gold say?" Mom wondered. She probably wanted to know if he figured out why I'm ruining her life. I told her that we just played chess for a while, which didn't thrill Dad too much. "I paid that man eighty dollars so you could play chess?" he asked. "I guess," I said, but then I thought his vein might start popping out, and I didn't feel like getting in a fight right before we had to leave for Parents' Night at school. So before anyone could scream at me, I ran up to my room. Besides, I couldn't wait to change out of that itchy mohair sweater.

# Absolute Delight

Parents' Night was totally phony. The teachers told all the parents that their kids are incredibly smart and hardworking and courteous, even the parents of the really dumb and lazy and nasty kids. Mr. Miller didn't even complain about how I won't say the Pledge of Allegiance anymore because there really *isn't* liberty and justice for all. Instead he told Mom and Dad that I'm an absolute delight. "A bit too compulsive maybe, but an absolute delight. An absolute delight." He said it twice like that, in case Mom and Dad didn't hear it the first time.

Then all these parents came up to us and started talking about how proud Mom and Dad must be of me. They were talking about how I won the middle school science contest and the Presidential Physical Fitness Award, how I got the lead role in the French play, and how my picture was posted in a clipping from the school newspaper because I came up with the "most unique" model for a town. I was hoping Mom wouldn't get mad at me for being unique again, but she didn't see that part because she was looking at my picture. "Why can't you look like your friends?" she asked, I guess because there was a picture of Leslie and Lana from the talent show next to mine. "They have such adorable little figures." I'd have to lose ten pounds to look like Leslie and Lana.

I couldn't stand being with all the adults, so I walked away and then I saw Leslie and everyone by the water fountain. But when I got close I could hear them talking about what everyone was wearing, and I hate talking about that. Besides, Leslie's still mad about the Presidential Physical Fitness Award, and she's turned everyone against me. So instead I went into the bathroom where I figured I'd sit on a toilet seat and draw chess strategies on the bottom of my sneakers, but Lana and Tracy were already there flipping their hair in front of the mirror. They were using all this hair spray, and when I tried explaining how it's bad for the air, Tracy turned and said, "No, *you're* bad for the air, Lori." Then she looked at Lana and they laughed like mad.

I obviously wasn't about to stay there, but I didn't have anywhere to go either. So I walked around the halls until I ended up by that trash can I always throw my lunches in before homeroom. The janitor already emptied the trash so all the parents would think our school is really clean, and I sort of wondered if the janitor ever noticed my lunch sitting in there. I kind of hoped he did, and that he gave it to someone who wanted it, but I doubted it. Then I couldn't stop thinking about the janitor and how I've never seen what he looks like because he comes after school. I mean, no one even knows he's alive. I'll bet he's as lonely as I am. It made me so sad thinking about how lonely we are that I almost started crying. But then I figured Mom and Dad might be wondering where I went, so I walked back to where all the parents were. Except they weren't looking around for me like I thought they'd be. They were too busy talking to Leslie's parents about fancy restaurants and stuff. They didn't even notice I was gone.

That's when I saw Fred Smuckler walk in with his mom. Fred is this incredibly nerdy kid with buckteeth, so I was pretty surprised he came to Parents' Night. I mean, he never even talks to anyone when he's at school, so I couldn't figure out why he'd want to come back to talk to nobody at night. He probably got dragged here by his parents, like I did. His mom was yelling at him because he lost his glasses in one of the classrooms and they were expensive. I never saw Fred without his gigantic glasses before, but he still looked incredibly nerdy. It wasn't at all like when Miss IQ took off her glasses and you found out she was pretty all of a sudden.

Anyway, Fred and his mom walked over to the wall where everyone's assignments were pinned up. I wanted to look at the assignments, too, but not when Fred was there. I didn't want Leslie starting a rumor about me talking to him, so I went to a different wall by my parents. But then the most embarrassing thing happened. Fred and his mom came up and started *standing* with us. You could tell Leslie got a big kick out of that. The reason they did this is that Fred's mom wanted to tell my parents how impressed she was with my typing assignment. She kept talking about how great it is that I already learned how to set the margins on business letters, because it's important for girls to know, just in case.

"In case of what?" I asked, but Fred's mom laughed and said I didn't have anything to worry about. "With a slender figure like yours, you won't have any trouble finding a husband," she said. "You'll probably get married before you even think about being a secretary." Like I'm planning on being a secretary my whole life if I don't get married. Then Mom noticed that where I wrote my name, "Lori," on the bottom corner of the assignment, some idiot changed it to "Hori." Real hilarious. I swear, everyone in my grade thinks they're Johnny Carson.

I know it sounds dumb, but all of a sudden I thought I might cry again. I was sick of being at Parents' Night, and I was sick of everyone at school. I guess Fred knew how I felt, though, because then he did the nicest thing. I couldn't believe it. He went over to his desk, took out a pencil, and came over to the wall to change my name back to "Lori." He didn't say one word when he did it either. I said thanks, and Fred kind of smiled back so you could see his buckteeth. That's when I heard Leslie laughing across the room. I knew she'd go and tell everyone that Fred was in love with me, or even worse, that I was in love with him, but I almost didn't care anymore. I even wondered if Leslie was the one who wrote "Hori," or if she put Lana up to it. Believe me, Lana would do *anything* Leslie wanted. She'd probably go off her diet if Leslie said to.

We went home pretty soon after that, thank God. But when I was walking upstairs, Dad noticed my typing assignment hanging out of my pocket. I tried to put it back in, but then the other assignment I took off the wall fell out by accident. It was Leslie's history assignment, which was supposed to be on the woman's suffrage movement, but she did it on Susan B. Anthony's clothes, naturally. Because I was mad at her for writing "Hori," I crossed out "Leslie" and wrote "Puslie" on the bottom of her assignment, but later I felt bad about it, so I took it down. Dad wasn't too happy about that. He said that first thing tomorrow morning, he's calling Dr. Gold because he isn't paying someone to play chess with me when I have a big problem with stealing other people's property. I wonder if he's also planning on telling Dr. Gold about Mr. Miller calling me "an absolute delight," but I doubt it. I don't think Dad heard that part, even though Mr. Miller said it twice.

# Don't Talk with Your Mouth Full

Dad called Dr. Gold to tell him what happened at Parents' Night, and Dr. Gold said we should go in for a family session. I guess Dad couldn't find all the answers he needed about me in *The Golden Cage.* He read the whole book in one night, then he gave it to Mom, but she was more interested in reading one of her sappy romance books. So I asked Mom if I could borrow *The Golden Cage,* and she said okay since it might take her a while to get to it. She was happy we bought it, though. "At least someone understands what I'm going through," she said. She was pretty excited about that.

I was excited to read *The Golden Cage* because it's written by a doctor named Hilde Bruch. I was hoping that since Hilde's a woman, she'd say how normal it is for women to diet. It turned out to be an incredibly stupid book, though, mostly because it said the whole reason I'm not eating is because I don't want to grow up. Which is totally wrong. I can't wait to grow up so it'll be normal to diet.

The only part I liked was when Hilde told stories about teenagers named Kate, Hazel, and Karla who felt as lonely as I do. There was even this one girl named Celia who had a mother just like mine. Hilde said that Celia's mother "behaved in an exceedingly childish way." I liked reading about these girls because they were interested in painting and music and books and math, unlike Leslie and Lana. Plus they did smart things like wear weights under their sweatpants for their weight checks, and some even threw up after they ate so none of the calories would be digested. Believe me, I never would have thought of that.

Dad's office is one block away from Dr. Gold's office, so Mom, David, and I met Dad in the waiting room for the appointment. We were early, so Dad pulled out his *Wall Street Journal,* Mom filed her fingernails, and David leaned against the wall so Mom and Dad could take the chairs. I swear, David's such a kiss-up.

I got pretty bored waiting, so I started going over the lines in my head for this French play I'm in at school. I play a rabbit called Janot Lapin, who's the leader of a group of farm animals. It's not the most interesting play in the universe, but we only know three verb tenses so far so we didn't have a lot of choices. There's this one scene where I'm really hungry because the landowners aren't feeding us, and I keep saying, *"J'ai faim."* In case you don't know, that means "I'm hungry," but it really means "I have hunger." That's what real French people say. I think it's neat how French people *have* hunger, but they *aren't* hungry like Americans are. I mean, it's a lot easier to try not to have something than to try not to be it.

I practiced my lines for a long time before Dr. Gold finally called us into his office. I sat in a leather chair kind of like Dr. Gold's, David took the other chair, and Mom and Dad were left with the giant couch. They looked pretty uncomfortable being on a psychiatrist's couch. Dad kept shifting around, and Mom kept crossing and uncrossing her legs so much I thought she might snag her panty hose, which definitely would have made her cry. Then Dr. Gold smiled and thanked everyone for coming in, and I worried for a second that he might never stop smiling, just like the last time.

But Dr. Gold surprised me. He came right out and asked Mom and Dad to talk about why things aren't going so well in our house. Then Mom and Dad looked at each other and decided to let Dad talk, probably because he answers all the "why" questions in our family. "Well, doctor, we honestly don't know why Lori's acting this way," he said, even though Dr. Gold asked about our *whole* house, not just me. I always get blamed for things. Then he said that everything was fine until I started my ridiculous diet in Washington, and that he never thought I could be so stubborn. Look who's talking! Dad's King Stubborn. At least *I* don't go around making people sit at restaurants on vacation until they eat their potato salad.

But Dr. Gold just nodded a bunch of times, and you could tell Dad wasn't too thrilled about that. He was probably waiting for Dr. Gold to give him a plan to make me eat, like those prescriptions Dr. Katz always writes out: "Drink Whole Milk," "Buy *The Golden Cage*," "Food is medicine." Dr. Gold kept smiling, though, so Dad came right out and asked him what my problem is. "Do you think it has something to do with the changes she's going through?" he asked. It always makes David and me laugh when Dad calls puberty "changes," so we made sure not to look at each other. Then Dad explained how David never did anything crazy when he went through his "changes," but how I've always been a sensitive kid and maybe I feel things too deeply. "Do you think that's the problem, doctor?" Dad asked.

Instead of answering, Dr. Gold asked Dad a new question: "What do you think your daughter's feeling?" But Mom butted in pretty fast. "She's thinking about math and calories all the time," Mom said. "Do you think you can help her?" Like being interested in math is some terrible mental problem. Then she started tearing up and reached for some tissues. Dr. Gold keeps big boxes of tissues in his office, probably so all the ladies on diets can keep their mascara from running.

Luckily, Dr. Gold didn't want to talk about my math problem. He was still interested in knowing if Dad knew what I was *feeling,* not thinking. Then Dad said he had no idea what I was feeling, other than fat, which he can't understand at all. "No one can understand it. Just look at her!" Mom yelled, pointing at me. She wouldn't stop butting in, so Dr. Gold asked Mom if she had any idea why I was feeling fat, but she didn't want to answer that question. Mom was much more interested in talking about what *she* was feeling.

Mom said she was feeling sad because she and Dad give me the best advantages, but even the best advantages can't help if something's wrong with me. "You do everything you can, you give them braces so they'll have straight teeth, you drive them around day in and day out to doctors for their shots, or dance lessons for their posture, or shopping so they'll look nice. You do *everything*—but no matter how hard you try, your child's still abnormal." Mom was crying so hard she almost couldn't talk anymore, but she kept trying anyway. "We're not *prepared* for this . . ." she said, then she got all emotional and had to stop talking. She just kept pointing my way so Dr. Gold would know that the "this" she wasn't prepared for was me, in case he couldn't figure that out.

I thought Dr. Gold would finally see how nervous Mom gets, but I guess he's not a very good psychiatrist. He even told Mom that he understood how painful this must be for her, or something stupid like that. But at least Mom calmed down. Next it was David's turn to guess what I might be feeling. It was like we were on *Family Feud.* David shrugged and said he had no idea, except that lately I've been more of a moron than usual, just to get attention. "So your sister is feeling like she wants some attention?" Dr. Gold asked. Then David looked at Mom and Dad before he answered because, like I told you, he can be a pretty big kiss-up. "She always has to be the center of attention," David said, but this time Mom nodded instead of Dr. Gold.

Dr. Gold forgot to nod because he got very excited about what David said. He told us that none of us knew what anyone was feeling, and it was great that we were all communicating. Then he wanted me to communicate to the rest of the family what I was feeling, since they didn't know but were all very interested. Which is baloney, but I answered anyway.

"I'm feeling like everyone else in my family is crazy, and I'm feeling like it's unfair that I'm the one who has to see a shrink," I said. Then Dr. Gold sat up in his chair and told us that I was a great communicator, and that I was the only one in my family who used "I" statements and the word "feel" instead of "think."

That's when Dr. Gold gave us a big speech about communication and taught us how to practice it at home. "Thank you, doctor," Dad said when he shook Dr. Gold's hand after the session. I could tell Dad thought that all we needed to do was communicate for a week and I'd stop dieting. Then Mom gave Dr. Gold a big hug and said she felt really free all of a sudden because she won't have to hold anything inside anymore. Which makes no sense, because Mom always blurts out whatever she wants. David just said thank you and walked out. The last thing Dr. Gold told us before he closed the door was, "Remember to use 'I feel' statements."

When we got home, Dad went into his study to work and Mom went into the bedroom to call all her gossipy friends. David went straight to his bedroom and closed the door, but I could hear his stereo blasting Peter Frampton all the way downstairs. So much for communication. I went up to my room so I could figure out if those girls in *The Golden Cage* would weigh less than me if they were eight inches shorter, but no one weighed less than 55 pounds. Then I did a ratio for every single height, in case I grow taller or something. I kept multiplying out new ratios until I got called down to dinner.

The minute I walked into the kitchen, Mom said how much she liked Dr. Gold. You could tell she was madly in love with him, and she was pretty excited about communicating, too. "You know, Lori, I've been meaning to tell you something for a long time," she said. "It's about your hair. It really needs work. Your layers are all grown out, and you'd look just adorable with some wispy layers, especially around your face." Then she turned to Dad and said, "I love communicating!" I hate Dr. Gold.

I told Mom that Dr. Gold wanted us to say how we feel about *ourselves,* not about everyone else. That's why he spent all that time teaching us how to use "I feel" statements. "Okay, fine," Mom said. "*I feel* that your hair needs work. I'm just telling you how *I feel.*" Like I said, Mom always misses the point.


Dinner was brisket in a disgusting sauce, one of those frozen pea and carrot combinations, and fried potatoes dripping in oily gook. In the kitchen I dished out half a piece of brisket and scraped all the sauce off, then I blotted it with a paper towel, just in case I missed some. I learned that from my diet book called *Fun Fitness Tricks.* Then I put seven peas and eight carrot squares on my plate, but I didn't like the number eight because it sounds like "ate," so I took one off. I didn't go near those fried potatoes, obviously.

When I got to the table, Maria put little plates of salad in front of everyone's seat. Mom told me mine didn't have any dressing like it usually does because if I want to eat like a prisoner of war, she isn't worrying about it anymore. "I love communicating!" Mom kept saying. Then Dad said that he feels it's better to let the doctors take care of me because they're professionals and I need professional help.

No one would stop communicating, so I concentrated on my salad. I purposely ate only one crouton, and it took me four bites. Then I ate the dry lettuce, but I left one piece on the plate so I didn't feel like a pig for eating it all. Then I started playing this game where I had to leave one of everything on the plate—like one forkful of brisket, or one pea, or one of those carrot squares. I kept changing the rules, though, so I had to start leaving two of everything on my plate, then three of everything, then four. I couldn't stop changing the rules, so finally I decided to eat just one more bite of everything. I was saving the brisket for last.

The TV wasn't on during dinner like it usually is because Mom and Dad were so excited about communicating. They said every single sentence starting with "I feel," even things like, "I feel the brisket tastes delicious." It was just like Mrs. Rivers with her Power Paragraph Transition Words, except the only transition on this list was "I feel." Finally I said that everyone should just talk like normal people, because we all sounded like a bunch of morons.

"Use 'I feel,'" David said. He just wanted to get me in trouble, so I kicked him under the table and he kicked me back, which practically broke my leg. "Feel this!" I yelled and whacked him with my other foot. Then Dad said, "I feel that you two should stop fighting right this minute or you'll both get no TV for a week." That's when I gave David my meanest glare ever.

"Instead of making a sour face, Lori, express what you're feeling," Mom said. Dr. Gold obviously brainwashed my entire family. "You're all taking this communicating stuff way too far," I told them. "I don't feel we are," Dad said. "I don't feel that either," Mom said. Then I ate the bite of brisket I was saving for last and said, "Well, I do feel that," but Mom told me she felt it was rude to talk with my mouth full.

# Chewing on Air

I wanted to play chess with Dr. Gold again today, but instead he wanted to talk about my dreams. I haven't been sleeping much lately, so I couldn't remember if I even *had* a dream last night. Dr. Gold said that everyone has dreams, though, and if I'd just relax a little, I'd remember mine, too. Then he wanted me to lie down on the giant couch, but there was no way I was doing that. First of all, I'm not crazy, and second of all, you burn less calories lying down. So I sat in the chair and kept trying to think of my dreams, but I still couldn't remember any.

Instead I remembered the dream this girl named Ida had in *The Golden Cage*. Hilde thought Ida's dream was so great that she named the whole book after it. It was about Ida feeling like a sparrow in a golden cage, and how everything looked beautiful and golden around her, but she felt like she was trapped in a tiny birdcage. I kind of know how she feels, but I couldn't use Ida's dream because that would be what Mrs. Rivers calls plagiarism. Luckily, I finally remembered my own dream.

In the dream, I was driving a motorboat out in the ocean and the wind was blowing my hair all over the place, except it didn't matter because Mom wasn't there to yell at me about putting a scarf on my head. I was going really fast, and I was the only boat in the water, the only person left alive on earth, actually.

"Where were you going?" Dr. Gold asked, but I told him that if he kept butting in, I wouldn't tell him my dreams anymore. I mean, it's hard to remember your dreams anyway, but it's practically impossible if someone's giving you the third degree.

"So anyway," I said, "I was out there driving this boat, and I guess I knew I was the only person around. At first I was scared that I wouldn't be able to survive all alone, because there wouldn't be things like houses and food."

"Tell me more about the food," Dr. Gold said, but when I gave him a good glare, he whispered, "I'm sorry, go on." Except I kind of didn't feel like going on. I mean, if it was up to me, we'd be playing chess. I'll bet Dad told him that we aren't allowed to do that anymore.

"Anyway," I said, "I was getting worried about surviving alone, but then I realized that I'm sort of alone already. No one likes me anymore, other than my bird, Chrissy, so I'd be just fine living alone."

"Tell me more about that," Dr. Gold whispered, but then I said I wouldn't tell him more about anything, since he broke his promise. I told him that I didn't care if I lived all alone because no one understands a word I say, including him. So why should I waste my breath? That's when I remembered the best part of my dream—the part about my breath.

What happened was, I was driving along in the boat, but I couldn't see where I was going because the sun was in my eyes and I didn't have any sunglasses. But I wasn't scared because I knew that the boat was taking me to a safe place. I even started laughing, and that's when I opened my mouth and all this air blew in. The air tasted like everything mixed together—red plums and salty Fritos and strawberry jelly and creamy Oreos. It tasted like everything and nothing at the same time, like if you mix a bunch of paint colors in art class and the mixture turns black.

But the thing is, my mouth got so full of air that I thought my cheeks might explode. I almost couldn't breathe. I tried chewing the air so I could swallow, but it wouldn't go down. It just stayed there, and I thought I might die, so I kept on chewing harder and harder. Then all of a sudden I could breathe again, and I was full. But the best part of the dream was when this wave came along and carried my boat up to heaven. I wasn't scared about not surviving anymore, because obviously I survived just fine chewing on air.

I didn't look at Dr. Gold the whole time I was telling the dream because I was too busy trying to picture everything in my head. But when I looked again, his eyebrows were all scrunched up, and I could tell he didn't think my dream was as good as Ida's. I was sorry I told him about it after all. So I didn't tell Dr. Gold anything else because he talks to Dr. Katz, and yesterday Dr. Katz said that if I don't "shape up," they'll put me in the hospital. That was when I told Dr. Katz that I want to shape down, not up, but Dr. Katz said it's not funny because if I go in the hospital, it won't just be for half a day like when I got the GI test.

Tonight I was watching *Charlie's Angels* and wondering how much the Angels weigh and how they can run so fast in high-heeled strappy sandals, when Dad knocked on my door to see if I wanted to play a game of chess. I said I was watching *Charlie's Angels,* but since the skinny Angels were making me feel fat, I'd turn it off to play chess. Then Dad said that I'm much skinnier than all the Angels, but he stopped talking about it because he must have remembered that Mom and him aren't allowed to talk about my weight anymore. Dr. Gold won't let them.

But since Dad already brought it up, I told him that if I was really as skinny as the Angels, I wouldn't need to diet. "Look how skinny they are," I told Dad, and he didn't have any trouble looking at them either. He wouldn't stop looking at them running after some bald man for about ten blocks. I guess that's how the Angels stay so skinny—doing all that running and stuff. I told Dad that if the Angels, instead of fat people like Dr. Katz and Dr. Gold, said I was too thin, I'd believe *them.*

We didn't play chess after that because Dad went into his study and called an old fraternity brother of his who's editing a TV movie that Jaclyn Smith is starring in. This friend of Dad's said that Jaclyn Smith is one of the nicest people he's ever met, and he'll ask her if she'll meet me. But Dad said I better be serious about not dieting anymore if she says I'm too thin, or I'll really be in trouble. I'm not worried about getting in trouble, though, because there's no way that someone like Jaclyn Smith will say I'm too thin. I mean, it's not even possible.

# "Hello, Angels. . . . It's Charlie"

I guess being on TV makes you look shorter than you really are, because when I saw Jaclyn Smith in person, I didn't expect her to be so tall. I was pretty excited to meet her, though. I thought Dad would be excited, too, because of the way he kept looking at her on TV, but he acted like he didn't care. Dad doesn't get a big kick out of TV stars the way Mom does. Mom was more excited than me, practically.

"I can't wait to meet Jackie!" Mom kept saying. Dad's editor friend told us that everyone who's friends with Jaclyn Smith calls her Jackie, but Mom started calling her that before she even met her. "Don't you want to look nice when Jackie comes over?" Mom kept asking me yesterday. But when I told her to stop worrying about what I was wearing, Mom concentrated on what *she* was wearing. She tried on about ten different outfits this morning, just to meet Jaclyn Smith for five seconds. I mean, she wasn't even coming with us to lunch.

Jaclyn was supposed to pick me up at noon, so at 11:45, four of David's friends showed up at the front door. They left their bikes in the driveway, too, which always makes Mom mad. I told David that he better send his friends home, but he said he always has friends over on Saturdays and he couldn't care less if Jaclyn Smith was coming over. "Then why did you steal Mom's magazine with that picture of Jaclyn Smith on the cover?" I asked. I saw the magazine on David's stereo. That's when one of David's friends yelled, "Busted!" and I said, "You better not come downstairs and stare when Jaclyn gets here, or I'll take all the *Playboys* from under your mattress and show them to Mom and Dad!" But David just started walking away and said, "Like I care." I knew he did, though.

Then I went upstairs and waited at the window. It got to be about 12:10, but I kept waiting anyway, just in case Jaclyn had a very slow limo driver. I figured being a big TV star, she'd come in a limo. But she wasn't here at 12:15, and by 12:25 I didn't think she was coming after all, so I was about to go back to my room and forget about the whole thing. That's when I saw Mom pacing back and forth in the hallway, saying, "Where's Jackie? Where's Jackie?" over and over. She sort of reminded me of that Miss Havisham lady I read about in my Mentally Gifted Minors literature class. I was too scared to walk by her, so I went back to the window and thought about what a phony Jaclyn Smith was for saying she'd come when she wasn't planning on doing it in the first place. That's when I got out some stationery and starting writing to Samantha's dad at ABC so I could tell him what a terrible show *Charlie's Angels* is. First of all, real detectives don't wear slinky dresses and bikini tops, and second of all, if a show's named *Charlie's Angels,* you should at least get to see what *Charlie* looks like once in a while.

But I didn't send the letter, because at 12:30 Jaclyn's yellow Mercedes pulled up in front of our house. "She's here!" I shouted, and Mom ran to the window. Then we both watched the car door open. A long, skinny leg came out, then lots of beautiful dark hair, and finally, graceful as a real angel, Jaclyn Smith walked toward our house. I saw her look at all the bikes in the driveway, then I heard David and his friends run to the front door. It was like a stampede. I took off downstairs to stop them, but it was too

late because the doorbell rang. "I'm telling about the *Playboy*s!"
I yelled, then I opened the door.

I couldn't believe that Jaclyn Smith was standing in front of
me. "You must be Lori," she said, and I tried to leave before she
noticed David and his friends staring, but all of a sudden Mom
came to the top of the stairs. "Jackie, I'm Roz. Please come in,
won't you?" Mom said, but her voice was different. It sounded
like the voice of this soap opera actress she likes a lot. When I
looked up the staircase, I saw two beautiful legs and lots of dark
blow-dried hair. Then Mom practically tiptoed down each step
in her skinny high heels. I swear, Mom wasn't Mom anymore.
She was Charlie's fourth Angel: Kelly, Sabrina, Kris, and Roz.

The minute Jaclyn came inside, David and his friends stepped
back a little, like they were scared of her or something. Jaclyn said
hi to them, and they all looked down at the floor and mumbled
hi at the same time, except for Philip, who giggled like a retard.
What idiots. Then Mom kept thanking "Jackie" for taking me
out. I really wanted to get out of there before Mom called her
Jackie again, but Dad came downstairs. That was even more embarrassing. Dad shook Jaclyn's hand and said how nice it was to
meet her, and I'll bet it was, too. He wouldn't let go of her hand.


Finally we left for lunch. Jaclyn opened the car door for me and I
got into her Mercedes. I kind of expected to see the CB radio that
Charlie always calls the Angels on, but when Jaclyn started talking, I remembered that she's not that Kelly lady she plays on TV.
She asked me about *me*—what I like to do and what I'm interested in. I was glad she didn't ask something stupid like, "So, do
you have a boyfriend yet?" like all the other adults do. She didn't
even shake her head when I told her how we're all gonna die from
the sun because ladies use too much hair spray. All she said was
how she wishes they didn't use so much hair spray on *Charlie's
Angels,* and how she never uses it at home.

You'd think someone like Jaclyn Smith would want to eat in

one of those fancy restaurants in Beverly Hills, but we didn't go anyplace like that. Instead we went to a coffee shop. I usually worry a lot on Saturdays about not being able to throw my lunch away like I do at school, but today I was excited about going to lunch. I couldn't wait to see what someone as thin as Jaclyn Smith eats in real life. I mean, I've never seen the Angels eat anything on *Charlie's Angels*. All they do on that show is sit around in Charlie's office and look beautiful, or chase people.

It turns out that Jaclyn ordered a hamburger—not the diet-plate hamburger with no bun and low-fat cottage cheese and tomato slices on the side, but the regular hamburger. I figured 180 calories for the bun, 150 calories for things like pickles, lettuce, ketchup, and oil, and 245 calories for a three-ounce hamburger. I ordered a tuna salad with the dressing on the side, and I ate some of the lettuce. Jaclyn only ate about half of her hamburger, because she said it didn't taste very good. So I said the same thing about my tuna salad and luckily she didn't ask any questions, even though I was lying. I wondered if Jaclyn was lying, too, or if she really would have eaten the whole hamburger if it tasted good, but I doubted it.

After we were finished, Jaclyn and I went up to the counter to pay a guy named Bill. At least that's what his name tag said. But Bill said he was really an actor and only working at the restaurant between parts, which was obviously a bunch of baloney. He didn't look like any of the hunky guys Mom loves to watch on TV. You could tell he liked Jaclyn, though, because when she gave him the money, he held her hand the way they do in old movies where the man kisses the top part. But Bill never kissed her. He just said how unbelievable it was that such a beautiful woman didn't have a wedding ring on. Bill probably thought I would grow up to be a secretary, but he sure thought Jaclyn was thin enough to get married.

When we got in the car again, I told Jaclyn that the boys at my school don't flirt the way Bill did. Bill was gross when he flirted, but he was still being nice and complimenting her. I told Jaclyn how everyone says Chris likes me, but he's always making fun of me. Like every time Chris and Michael see me in the hallway, Michael says to Chris, "Isn't Lori pretty?" and Chris says, "Yeah, pretty brainy." Then they laugh like mad. At least Bill knew the right way to flirt with a woman, even if he was really a cashier and not an actor.

After lunch, we ended up going to Jaclyn's house for a while. When we walked in the front door, though, two huge black poodles came running toward us. Before I could move out of the way, one of them jumped on me and knocked me onto the floor, which hurt like mad. It felt like I broke my hipbone or something, but I told Jaclyn I was fine because you could tell she felt bad about it. "No one's ever gotten knocked over by the poodles before," she said. "You really are petite." I wondered if that was supposed to mean that Jaclyn thought I was too thin, but I didn't think it counted. Mrs. Rivers would say it was out of context.

Jaclyn gave me some ice for my hip and put the dogs in another room, then we sat around the living room and she told me how she became an actress, and about her family and her 101-year-old great-grandfather. We didn't talk about boring things like shopping. Before we left, I saw a bunch of boxes of pictures on the floor. They were pictures of Jaclyn, but not like the kind Mom takes in front of monuments. These were black-and-white head shots, and Jaclyn didn't even bother smiling in some of them. Mom always smiles like she just won a million dollars in all her pictures, even though one of her magazines said never to smile because you'll get wrinkles. Jaclyn saw me looking at the pictures and asked if I wanted one. I said I wanted the one where she isn't smiling, so she gave me that one plus two others. On the one I liked best she wrote, "Much love and happiness to my good friend Lori," which is funny, since no one else seems to want to be my friend lately.

It wasn't until we were driving back to my house that I re-

membered I still hadn't asked about whether I'm too thin or not.
I knew Dad would kill me if I forgot, but what I really wanted to
know is how Jaclyn stays so thin herself. So I told Jaclyn that all
the girls at school want me to bring back diet tips from her. The
truth is, no one at school even knows about our lunch, but I
thought the question might get Jaclyn talking about her diets,
then later I could bring up my weight. But Jaclyn didn't have any
diet tips because when she was a kid, she was so thin she had to
drink protein shakes all the time so she could *gain* weight. Except
she doesn't drink the shakes anymore because she said it's much
easier to gain weight as a woman. I'll bet that's the real reason she
only ate half of her hamburger at lunch.

We were almost at my house by this time, so I knew I had to
come right out and ask Jaclyn if she thought I was too thin. "You're
not too thin," she answered, but she didn't look at my body to
check. She was looking at the car in front of us and telling me how
everyone's body is different, and how if people say I'm too thin, I
should just ignore them. "We all develop at our own rate," she said.
I told her that I spent the last couple of months trying explain to
everyone that I'm not too thin, but no one will listen. And I said I
can't just ignore them because Dr. Katz will make me go to the hospital if I don't stop my diet and gain weight by next week.

"You're on a diet?" Jaclyn asked. This time she looked over
at my body. "Well, not really a diet, I just watch what I eat," I
answered. I thought she might start lecturing me about the diet
like everyone else does, but she just nodded and we didn't talk
anymore because we pulled up to my house. Then she invited
me to visit the set of *Charlie's Angels* when they start taping
again, and I said I'd go if they didn't put me in the hospital
first. But before I got out of the car, Jaclyn took my hand and
smiled. "I'd really love to teach you how to make those protein
shakes," she said. "We could make a day of it." She meant it,
too. She even gave me her private phone number.

• • •

David's friends' bikes weren't in the driveway anymore, thank God, but when I got to the front door, I heard a bunch of footsteps. I could tell that Mom and David watched us from the windows, even though they acted like they didn't hear me come in. David pretended to build a model, and Mom had a *Redbook* magazine on her lap. I started running after David for bringing all his friends over to see Jaclyn, but my hipbone still hurt, then Mom stopped me when she saw the autographed pictures in my hand. "Isn't Jackie beautiful?" she asked, and she got that dreamy look in her eyes she always gets when she watches her soap operas. "You have the same hair as Jackie," she said. "If only you'd style it more often, instead of wearing it in that ridiculous ponytail." I told Mom she could keep the pictures if she wanted, then I went upstairs.

Dad was up in his study, and the first thing he wanted to know was what Jaclyn said when I asked if I was too thin. "She said that everyone's body is different, and that if people say I'm too thin I should just ignore them," I answered, which was true, but Dad thought I was lying. He said she couldn't possibly say something like that because of how I look, and that even if I was telling the truth—and he doubted it—the only reason Jaclyn would say that is because she was being polite. Mom and Dad never told her about my "situation" because they thought it would be pretty obvious once she saw me.

I told Dad that Jaclyn doesn't say things just to be polite. She's not phony like that. But Dad explained how everyone's a little bit phony. It's called etiquette, he said, like I wasn't already taught that word a million times by Mom. I didn't like what Dad was saying about Jaclyn being a phony, so I asked how you can tell if someone really means something, or if it's just etiquette. "What she said about your weight, that was just etiquette," Dad answered. Then he shook his head and took a long puff from his pipe, which probably meant he thought the whole Jaclyn Smith plan to get me to eat was a total waste.

# E Is for Electrolyte

Tonight we all drove to Dr. Gold's office for what everyone kept calling an "emergency session." I didn't see what the big emergency was, but we were supposed to talk about my health. The minute we got there, though, I found out the *real* reason for the session. Dr. Gold said we needed to decide if I should go to the hospital. Since Dr. Gold always tells me he doesn't think I'm crazy, at first I figured I didn't have anything to worry about. But it turns out Dr. Gold tried to blame it all on Dr. Katz.

First Dr. Gold said that *Dr. Katz* is very concerned about my situation. He said that's because of all of the blood tests *Dr. Katz* keeps taking at my weight checks. *Dr. Katz* told Dr. Gold that my blood cell count and electrolyte levels aren't good, but when I asked Dr. Gold what electrolytes are, he didn't answer. He was too busy telling everyone how *Dr. Katz* said I lost another pound this week, and how *Dr. Katz* is very upset about this.

When Dr. Gold finished blaming Dr. Katz for everything, he wanted to know how we felt about the information. Mom perked up when she heard the word "feel." "I feel it would be best for Lori if the doctors take care of her in the hospital," she said. She loved using "I feel," especially in front of Dr. Gold. But Dr. Gold just nodded and turned to Dad. "Well, doctor, I want to do what's best for Lori," he said. He also wanted to know if the hospital takes our medical insurance. "Do you know, doctor, if anorexia nervosa is an accepted diagnosis?" I didn't know what was worse: Mom saying "I feel" all the time or Dad saying "doctor" every second. I was glad it was David's turn next. If anyone would stick up for me, it would be David. It's true we fight a lot lately, but we used to be best friends once. I knew in an emergency—and Dr. Gold called this an emergency session—I could count on him.

But David didn't say anything at first. He just gave me our funny look, which almost made me laugh. I figured he was probably scared of sticking up for me in front of Mom and Dad because he's such a big kiss-up, but he'd get the nerve in a minute or so. I mean, I'd even say nice things about *Leslie* if someone wanted to put her in a hospital, and I can't stand her now.

"David, the doctor is talking to you," Dad said, but David just kept looking at the floor. Then Dr. Gold told David that anything he says is okay because it's important as a member of the family to express his opinion and communicate. So all of a sudden David blurted out, "I think she should go to the hospital. She's making everyone nervous." I couldn't believe it! That's when I figured out that the whole session was a big setup, and that everyone knew they were sending me to the hospital before we even got there. What traitors.

I told Dr. Gold that there never was any emergency, but he tried acting very innocent, like he wasn't in on the plot. Instead he asked me how I felt about what everyone said, but I wouldn't look at him because I thought I might start crying. I kept wondering what electrolytes are, and if they're like electricity, how come they haven't electrocuted me yet since I drink eight tall glasses of water each day. I sort of wanted to be electrocuted right then. But Dr. Gold was still staring at me, so finally I said I'd do anything—go to high school early, go away to boarding school if I made everyone too nervous—*anything*, if I didn't have to go to the hospital. I kept thinking about the girl at Children's Hospital, in the purple baseball hat with no hair underneath, and I got scared about staying at a hospital overnight and sleeping next to bald kids. I promised I'd do anything, just *please* don't make me go to the hospital.

Then Dr. Gold wanted to know what I meant by "anything." He asked if it meant eating, but I never meant that. When I said "anything," I meant anything I could *do*. I can't eat if I'm this fat. It was obviously a trick question. But before I could answer, Dad told Dr. Gold that we went through this before, when I promised to eat and then I didn't. He started telling the Jaclyn Smith story, but I said I only promised to eat if Jaclyn Smith said I was too thin, and she never said that. Etiquette or no etiquette. Dad kept telling the whole story anyway, though, probably so he could think about Jaclyn some more.

That's when Dr. Gold's light went on, which meant we had to go. Before we left, Dr. Gold told me that I have to go to the hospital, but only because everyone cares so much. Baloney. I mean, I don't see other parents sending their kids to the hospital because they care so much. Then Dr. Gold said he'll call Dr. Katz tomorrow and make all the arrangements for me to go to a pediatric unit on Tuesday, the day after the Memorial Day holiday, but I'll bet everything was already arranged days ago. Mom didn't even ask if she'd have to chauffeur me to the pediatric unit, probably because she's in on the plot, too. She must be happy she won't have to chauffeur me anywhere while I'm away.

When Dr. Gold walked us all to the door, I asked him why I had to come to the emergency session if no one listened to my opinion anyway. I told Dr. Gold he was a liar and a traitor, but he just kept saying that we'll talk about it later, and that he cares a lot about my opinion. "Why, Lori, we all feel that your opinion is extremely valuable," he said, even though he didn't feel it was extremely valuable five minutes before. "That's just etiquette!" I yelled, but Mom and Dad made me leave.

On the way home, Dad kept reading every single street sign and store name out loud, even though Dr. Gold's office is only a few blocks from our house and Dad sees these signs every day. It's a habit Dad has. "Wilshire Boulevard," "Saks Fifth Avenue," "No Left Turn." I swear, he wouldn't stop. I used to play a game like that with David when we were little kids and our family would drive down to San Diego for vacation. The rule was, you had to find a word on a street sign that started with the last letter of the word the other person just called out. But you always tried to get a word that started or ended with a vowel because those were really hard to find. The best words, though, were the ones that started *and* ended with a vowel. We called those "winner words."

But that was before, when David still liked me. I tried to remember the last time we played that game, but I couldn't think because Dad kept calling out more signs. "No Parking," "Right Lane Must Turn Right." It was really bugging me, but Dad wouldn't stop. Maybe he always wanted to be a famous announcer instead of a stockbroker. "Rodeo Drive," "The Beverly Wilshire," he said. Finally I figured I'd try playing the game by myself, so I looked for a sign that started with "e," since "Wilshire" ends with "e." I didn't see one, but all of a sudden I thought of a word that has an "e" at the beginning *and* end. A winner word.

"Electrolyte!" I shouted, then my whole family turned their heads and looked at me like I'm nuts. I'll bet they can't *wait* to send me away to the hospital.

# 3:
## Summer 1978

# Breck Girl

The hospital I'm at is called Cedars-Sinai, and luckily it's not too far from our house because Dad called out street signs the whole way over. Then Mom kept telling Dad how to drive, and Dad kept running lights because he hates being late. All this gave me a terrible headache by the time we got to the hospital. I actually couldn't wait to go inside so a doctor could give me some aspirin.

Cedars is a really nice place, though, as far as hospitals go. Mom said a lot of movie stars deliver their babies and get face lifts here, but that's in the South Tower. I'm in the pediatric unit, which is in the North Tower. The minute we got here, the receptionist gave Dad a bunch of forms to fill out, and we all sat down in the waiting area. Then Mom pulled a romance book out of her purse, Dad grabbed a pen from the pocket inside his suit, and I peeked over Dad's shoulder to see what he was writing about me.

All the forms had their own names, and the first was called "Patient Information." Right underneath, it said that everything you write will be kept "strictly confidential." Except then in smaller letters, it said that anyone on the "treatment team" and anyone at the insurance company can see the records, but they'll also keep the information "strictly confidential." Then in even *smaller* letters, it said if you're a minor, like me, the information can be shared with the school, my parents, and anyone my parents feel like showing it to. So none of it sounded "strictly confidential" to me. After a bunch of questions about my address, phone number, doctor, age, height, and weight—which Dad left blank—there was a space called "Reason for Admission." Dad left that space blank, too. I told him to write "diet," since that's why I'm here, but Dad still left it blank, which is probably good. I mean, the truth is, nothing's wrong with me.

When Dad finally finished filling out all the forms, a nurse took us to my room. Everyone wears name tags here, and hers said ELIZABETH. She put a shiny plastic ID bracelet on my wrist, even though I hate wearing jewelry because it always gets in the way when you're trying to write essays or play sports. But Elizabeth said I had to wear the bracelet anyway—it's the law.

While Dad was outside talking to the insurance lady, Mom unpacked the sweatpants from my suitcase, and a bunch of doctors kept coming in and asking me the same questions over and over. The doctors are really medical students who said they had to practice taking histories on me, but I didn't feel like repeating everything a million times. So finally I asked the one named Doug if he could bring me some aspirin before my head exploded, but he never brought me any aspirin. He just wrote "headaches" on my chart, then he left and came back with Mike, who asked why I didn't tell him about the headaches in the first place. Mike said it was important to tell the truth because they were just trying to help me.

I told Mike that I'm here because of a diet, not a headache, but he wouldn't write down "diet" on the chart. He said that in a few hours he would find out the "real" reason from Dr. Katz, so I might as well be honest. I kept telling Mike I'd bet him a thousand dollars that Dr. Katz will say I'm here because of a diet, and then he'll feel sorry for calling me a liar, but this time

Mike wrote "uncooperative" on the chart. "I'm not uncooperative, there's really nothing wrong with me," I tried explaining,
but then Mom butted in and said, "Oh, please. She has anorexia
nervosa. A severe case."

That's when Mike and Doug looked at each other and sort of
shrugged. I figured they were probably absent for the anorexia
nervosa unit in medical school, so I told them to hand me their
charts and I'd write out the words for them. I know how to
spell it from *The Golden Cage.* I also crossed out the word "uncooperative" on Mike's chart and changed it to "absolute delight," but I don't think anyone noticed.

The second they left, Mom asked, "Aren't they cute? The
tall one's just adorable." I figured she was talking about Doug,
since he was pretty tall, but all I could remember about him
were the pimples on his forehead. "He's okay," I said, but then
she told me that unless I do something about my figure, I'll
never find anyone like Doug to marry. Like I'm worried about
marrying Doug. I mean, I'm *much* more worried about missing
my math test today.


The doctors made Mom and Dad leave before lunchtime, which
in this hospital is at 11:00. They kissed me good-bye, and when
Mom started crying, Dad took a hankie out of his suit pocket so
Mom could wipe her tears. I figured she wouldn't be needing me
to get tissues for her anymore. Then Mom and Dad left, and I
got scared all of a sudden. It all started when I smelled the trays
of food from the cart in the hallway, and I knew they'd be bringing one in for me. Then I noticed that you can't open any of the
windows in my room, which meant all the steam from the food
would be going straight into my stomach. I really wanted to go
home, so I tried running down the hall after Mom and Dad, but
Elizabeth grabbed me from behind.

"Where do you think you're going?" she asked. I started
yelling for Elizabeth to let me go, but she just held me until I

stopped trying to squirm away. Then she walked with me back to my room, but she stayed behind me the whole time so I couldn't turn around and run away again. She said that she's from Connecticut, so she understands what it's like to be away from your parents. I asked if her parents ever kicked *her* out of the house for dieting, but then I felt bad for asking. Elizabeth doesn't look like she ever diets, but maybe that's because her nurse's uniform is white and Mom's magazine said wearing white makes you look fat. It said never to wear white, except on your wedding day. You won't look fat that day because you have to diet for six months to fit into your wedding dress in the first place.

Elizabeth didn't answer, so on the way back to my room, I kept looking in all the other kids' rooms. Most were lying in bed and were hooked up to machines. Elizabeth saw me looking into the rooms and told me not to worry because everyone at the hospital will make sure I get healthy enough so I won't end up like those kids. I tried explaining that obviously I won't get hooked up to machines because I shouldn't even be here. I told Elizabeth I'm so healthy that when I first turned eleven I was asked to do a commercial for Breck shampoo. My line was, "My hair's so healthy!" and I was supposed to play some beautiful lady's daughter, but I never did because I didn't want to miss two days of school. "I could have been a Breck Girl, you know," I told Elizabeth. But then I saw something awful.

Doug and Mike were wheeling a kid down the hall, but I couldn't tell if the kid was a boy or a girl because it was bald, and half the kid's face looked like it was cut off. I kept staring at the kid, but Elizabeth didn't seem to notice. She just said that when I first turned eleven, my hair was healthy because I weighed more, but I can't be a Breck Girl anymore because I'm sick. "Didn't you see that kid?" I asked. "*That's* what sick looks like!" But all Elizabeth answered was, "Sick looks like a lot of things, Lori. This may surprise you, but you look sick to a lot of people, too."

# Fractions

According to Dr. Katz, these are the rules:

1. I get weighed every morning, facing away from the scale. The doctors will tell me when I come close to my "target" weight. (But they won't tell me what my target weight is.)

2. As I come close to my target weight, I'll get "privileges"—like I'll get to choose my own menu, or have visitors, or look in a full-length mirror. (Dr. Katz doesn't know that if I stand on the couch by the window after dark, I can see myself in the glass.)

3. A nurse has to sit with me during meals, and she won't go away until I eat 75% of what's on my tray.

4. I'm not allowed to drink eight tall glasses of water each day because everything I drink has to have calories. (They won't give me a cup for the bathroom, and I can't drink from my hands because the soap I use might have calories, too.)

5. If I exercise, I'll be punished. (But they won't tell me what my punishment is.)

6. I can't leave the ward unsupervised. (But until I eat, I'm not allowed to leave the ward supervised, either.)

Boarding school would have been better than this.

When Dr. Gold showed up yesterday, I told him that these rules won't make me eat. First of all, I need to pick my own menu, because at lunch they put things like avocados on my plate, and I didn't even eat those before I knew I was fat. I said if they'd just put a banana on my tray, I might eat that, which is better than nothing, so Dr. Gold told the other doctors I could pick my menu. That's why Bonnie came to my room last night.

"Hi! I'm Bonnie, the nutritionist!" she said. Bonnie wears short skirts and low-cut tops just like Miss Drabin. She must exercise a lot, too, because you can see her leg muscles through her panty hose. She bugged me right away because she says everything in a really excited voice, like she's talking to a puppy. Then she took out a bunch of colored charts showing the four food groups, but all the foods had cartoon bubbles sticking out of them saying stupid things like, "I'm good for you!" and "I make you grow!" I didn't like Bonnie very much, especially when she held up a picture of smiling bananas and dancing pancakes that said, "Let's boogie!"

Bonnie also had charts of what girls my age and height should weigh, and how many calories they're supposed to eat each day, but I didn't pay too much attention because I already saw those things in Dr. Katz's office. So when Bonnie was talking, I kept reading this great book about a sad French lady named Madame Bovary who's bored like me with everyone. But Bonnie took the book away and gave me some forms to fill out. I'm telling you, they love forms at this hospital.

The first form was called a Food Diary. It's divided into meal sections so you can write down everything you eat each day. I told Bonnie that I already keep a food diary, and I went into my backpack to show it to her. I explained how in my food diary, I write down all the foods I *don't* eat, but used to before I started my diet. I mean, I like to keep track of how much I've improved. I was hoping that keeping my own food diary would get me out of keeping Bonnie's, but she just told me that my behavior has to change. That's why she took out another diary.

This other diary is called my Behavior Modification Diary. Bonnie said that in this diary I'm supposed to write down behaviors I want to work on. I have to write down all my good and bad behaviors around food, and then I'm supposed to try to change the bad ones. Except there's a catch. The catch is, if I change the bad behaviors I'll get a reward, like having visitors, but if I don't, I'll get punished, like not having visitors until I'm twenty. I obviously didn't want to keep that diary, so I told Bonnie that I already do my own behavior modification. It's true, I've been doing it for months. The way mine works is, if I don't eat, I reward myself by getting to sleep extra late, and if I do eat, I punish myself by exercising double my normal amount. But Bonnie said I still have to keep her stupid diary.

That's when Bonnie started writing something on the chart I couldn't see, probably how I'm "unique" or "uncooperative" or something. Then she left me with the diary and a menu card to fill out. The behavior diary was fill-in-the-blank, like, "While I'm in the hospital, behaviors I'd like to work on include _____." I wrote, "None, *my* behavior isn't the problem. *I'm* not the one carrying around pictures of dancing pancakes." Another said, "I would like to communicate to the staff _____." I wrote, "How I've been asking for aspirin for two days and no one seems to care. What kind of hospital is this, anyway?" Then I thought Dr. Gold might want me to use "I feel" in the question about communication, so I drew an arrow after that and wrote, "I feel I should be able to get some aspirin in a big, fancy hospital like this." After that I wasn't in the mood to fill in any more blanks on that form, so I moved on to the menu card.

Bonnie said I have to pick something from each of the four food groups for every meal, and I have to eat a total of 2500 calories per day—which is how many I normally eat in a week. She even gave me a list of calories so I could make sure I was getting all 2500, like I didn't already memorize the calories in every food in the universe when I went to the school library at lunch. Besides, I brought *My Calorie-Counting Companion* with me, since it said to bring it with you everywhere you go. For breakfast, I ended up checking off a banana and Special K.

But when breakfast came today, they also put an omelet, bacon, whole milk, and sugary orange juice on my tray. So much for Dr. Gold saying I could choose my own menu. I swear, you can't trust Dr. Gold for one second. Elizabeth had to sit with me at breakfast, but she was flipping through a magazine the whole time. I normally like to eat alone, but since Elizabeth wasn't looking, I finally ate my banana and most of my Special K. Then Elizabeth said that she couldn't leave until I ate 75% of what was on my tray. I told her I didn't remember writing, "buttery omelet" or "greasy bacon" on my menu card, and if they gave me only the stuff I checked off in the first place, I would have eaten 100% of what was on my tray. I mean, I ate the banana and the cereal. I thought Elizabeth might start shaking her head at me like Bonnie did, but instead she sort of smiled. Then she scrunched her lips together so she'd look very serious and said that I really did need to eat 75% of what was on my tray because Dr. Katz will get mad if I don't, and he's coming at 3:30.

I told Elizabeth I couldn't eat because the food was gross. "I mean, would you eat this?" I asked. I was pointing at the oily omelet, and I was sort of being sarcastic, but then all of a sudden Elizabeth picked up the fork from my tray and took a big bite of the omelet. No wonder she looks fat in white.

"Umm, it's good," she said. She was holding out the fork for me, like I'd really eat off someone else's fork. I told Elizabeth that if she told Dr. Katz I didn't eat the omelet, I'd tell on her for taking a bite of my food, but that made her laugh. "Go ahead," she said. "We'll see who gets in more trouble." Which was a pretty funny thing for an adult to say. I mean, most adults don't know how to be sarcastic, or if they do, they aren't funny about it or anything.

I couldn't decide if I was still mad at Elizabeth, so I turned away from the tray and flipped on the TV they have hanging from the ceiling. Elizabeth didn't care, though, even when I made fun of all the actors on the commercials. She even laughed at the Palmolive lady who soaked her hands in dishwashing soap, which I have to admit, was pretty funny. But then she stopped joking around because she was busy looking at the little plastic containers on my tray so she could figure out what percentage of the meal I ate. She kept talking about how she was really bad at math in school, and how it was hard for her to become a nurse because of it. Then she told me she'd been working for twenty-four hours straight and was too tired to think, so she asked me to tell her how much 75% was. "Is that two-thirds or three-fourths?" she wanted to know. "It's half," I lied, so Elizabeth wrote in the chart that I ate a little under 75% of my breakfast.


After Elizabeth left, I was reading about how Madame Bovary lived with her boring husband named Charles who didn't understand her. Charles was a doctor, but he was a terrible one because he got someone's leg infected and they had to amputate it. Some doctor. Madame Bovary wanted to leave him, obviously, but she couldn't because she was a woman. I was right at the part where Madame Bovary started having an affair with a guy named Leon when Doug showed up.

Doug came in and said that he read about anorexia nervosa last night. I could tell he read Hilde's book, because he put his hand on my shoulder and told me that it must feel awful to be trapped in a cage. I explained to Doug how it was just a metaphor and how he shouldn't become a psychiatrist or he'll end up as dumb as Dr. Gold, but Doug said he's thinking more about becoming a dermatologist. That's when I went into the bathroom and got him some pimple cream Mom bought me before I came here, in case I get a blemish. I told him to put a little dab on each pimple twice a day, and that I'd let him keep the entire tube if he'd bring me some aspirin. I still had a headache, and my stomach hurt, too.

When Doug finally came back with the aspirin, he had white pimple cream all over his forehead. I told him that if he rubbed it in, it would turn clear, and if he didn't know that already, he should think about something besides being a dermatologist. Then he noticed I had my chessboard laid out on my bed. I was playing against myself, which isn't too fun in a game where the whole point is to try to outsmart the other person. So Doug said he had to do his rounds, but he'd play a very quick game which, if you know anything about chess, usually lasts at least an hour. He must have thought I'd be terrible at chess, like the boys in PE thought about girls who play softball.

It actually was a quick game, though, because I beat Doug in four moves, which didn't make him too happy. I was thinking that maybe Doug shouldn't try to become *any* kind of doctor, but I didn't say so. First of all, I felt bad for him with all that pimple cream on his face and second of all, I didn't want to play chess all alone. The truth is, I was really lonely. So Doug pushed the pieces off the board and started to set up a new game. "Two out of three?" he asked, but I hate losing, and I wanted better odds. "No, three out of four," I said, but Doug knows his fractions and only agreed to two out of three. Thank God they don't make *him* sit with me at meals.

# Brownie

Before my appointment with Dr. Gold today, Dr. Katz came in my room to talk to me alone. He took two tongue depressors out of his white coat, but he couldn't find anything to drum them on, so he put them back and sighed. His breath smelled like mouthwash for once. "This isn't a vacation, darlin'," he told me. Then he went on about how all I do is play chess and read books and watch *Charlie's Angels* reruns, and how I even set up an easel in the corner for the art projects the arts and crafts lady gave me, and how I'm living every kid's dream of not going to school and playing all day. "That's not what you're here for, darlin'," he said. *Duh.*

Dr. Katz was talking in his very serious tone just so I'd know how serious he was being. "You're here because you're sick, Lori. This is a hospital and you're acting like it's a hotel." I told Dr. Katz that it's such a nice hospital it sure looks like a hotel, but in a hotel, they don't put you next to sick kids who scare you half to death, they don't make you fill out behavior diaries, they don't wake you up before it's light out to take your temperature, they don't stick you with needles every day, they let you see your parents, they don't punish you for being on a

diet or exercising, and they don't make you stay inside a room
with windows that won't open when it's beautiful and sunny
out. So of course I read and watch *Charlie's Angels* and do art
projects—what else am I supposed to be doing while I'm sitting
here all alone in a hospital room? Dr. Katz was about to answer,
but I kept talking. "Most of all," I said, "if this was a hotel, I'd
be allowed to go to school and do my homework, and there's
nothing I'd rather do more than get my homework done!"
That's when Dr. Katz said he was sending Dr. Gold in right
away.

Dr. Gold came in and told me that even though I asked to
pick my own meals, I can't do that anymore since I keep losing
weight. "That was a privilege I granted you, and I feel you've
abused it," he said. Dr. Gold doesn't talk much, but when he
does, he always uses "I feel" statements. He said that as soon as
I gain weight, I'll be able to pick my own menus again, and I'll
also be able to have visitors. If I gain enough weight, I'll get to
go back to school. "I really feel it's your choice, Lori," he said.
Some choice: Be fat and go to school, or be thin and live with
dying kids.


When Dr. Gold finally left, a nurse whose name tag said
BROWNIE came in with a big bird full of candy and some balloons. The gift was from Erica and her mom, Sheila, and it
came with a note in Erica's writing. Erica wrote that she hoped
the bird would make me miss Chrissy less while I'm away. It
was a really nice gift, but I obviously didn't want all that sugar
smelling up my room. So I told Brownie to take the bird away,
but she wouldn't do it. "How can you give away *candy?*" she
asked. I didn't see what the big deal was, but then Brownie told
me that the reason she likes being called Brownie has nothing
to do with the color of her skin. It's because she loves sweets,
especially brownies. Brownie said that if she ever found out she

was dying, she'd just eat brownies all day and night until the very end. If you want my opinion, anyone who names herself after her favorite food is a hundred times weirder about eating than people say I am.

Brownie finally agreed to take the candy bird away and give it to the other kids, but first she took a handful of candies and tossed them into the pocket of that white nurse's outfit she wears. Brownie doesn't look fat in white like Elizabeth does. She's tall and skinny, even though she loves candy so much. I guess she wasn't cursed with slow metabolism either. After Brownie took the candies, she opened my door to leave, and that's when I smelled the dinner trays being rolled down the hallway. Then Brownie came back with my tray. I asked where Elizabeth was, but Brownie said she's off until Friday. I really wanted Elizabeth to sit with me instead, and not just because she can't do fractions. The truth is, Elizabeth makes me feel less lonely.

Unlike Elizabeth, Brownie didn't read magazines while I ate. She was too busy shoving little pieces of candy into her mouth and looking through my chart. She made lots of noise unwrapping each piece, but I tried not to pay too much attention because I was working hard on cutting up my food so it would look like I ate 75%. Trust me, it's not easy. But then Brownie asked, "What kind of disease do you have, child?" I told Brownie I don't have a disease, I just can't eat fattening things like sugar. That's when Brownie said, "Well then, why didn't they just write 'diabetes' on your chart instead of all this nonsense? Doctors!" You could tell Brownie didn't like doctors very much.

I said I didn't know why, but since I felt kind of dizzy, I asked if she would please just write down that I ate my 75% so I could take a nap. Then Brownie said she was sorry for making a big deal about the candy. She said she didn't know I had diabetes, and that I should eat something so I don't lose more weight. Then she looked in the chart to find out why she was supposed to be sitting with me at meals, but I guess she couldn't read Dr. Katz's messy writing either. She finally gave up and said if I didn't tell anyone, she'd leave me alone, even though I should try to be around other people. "I've seen my share of sick kids, child, and they're a whole lot happier if they meet the others. It ain't fun being sick alone." Before Brownie left, she told me I should go meet Nora, the girl in the next room, when I was done eating. Like I was really planning on eating.

The minute Brownie closed the door, I flushed most of my dinner down the toilet, just like we used to do to our goldfish when they would die. Then I tried watching TV, but all the families just made me miss being home. I was feeling pretty lonely for a long time, so finally I figured I'd go next door and see who Nora was. I heard Nora's fifteen, but when I saw her from the hallway, she looked a lot older. I never got to meet her, though, because Brownie came back and told me to go to my room, which made no sense since it was her idea for me to meet Nora in the first place.

"You lied to me about having diabetes," Brownie said when we got into my room. I tried explaining that I didn't lie, I just didn't say anything when *she* said I had diabetes. But Brownie wasn't only mad about me lying, she was also mad because she felt bad for me, and now it turns out that the only thing wrong with me is that I need to eat. She said most kids are here because they can't help being sick, but I'm here because I'm making myself sick on purpose. I tried explaining that I only want to make myself *thin,* not *sick,* but she just went over and looked at my tray to see how much food was gone. I saw her write down that I ate 85%. Brownie may know her fractions, but she sure didn't know about me flushing my food down the toilet.

After Brownie took the tray away, I figured she wasn't planning on coming back to keep me company. I mean, she really hated me. So I got down on the floor behind my bed to do some leg-lifts, but then something happened in the middle of my fifth set. I was counting the dots in the carpet when I saw these two white nurse's shoes step in front of me. They were the whitest shoes I've ever seen, and they must be pretty quiet, too, because all of a sudden I looked up and saw Brownie standing over me. She was holding the candy bird I got from Erica, and all she said was, "I think you oughta be more thankful for the gifts you get." She didn't even tell me to get up off the floor or punish me for doing the leg-lifts. She just put the candy bird in the spot where her shoes used to be, then she walked back out in her quiet shoes.

# Camp Cedars

Dr. Gold told Mrs. Rivers how nervous I've been about missing so much school, so Mrs. Rivers said I could do the final essay assignment from the hospital. I told Dr. Gold that I wasn't writing any more Power Paragraphs, but he said that's okay because all the assignment sheet said is that I have to compare two unlikely things. Here's my "Comparison Assignment":

When I was walking around the ward with Elizabeth today, I was thinking about how Dr. Katz said I'm acting like the hospital's a hotel, but it's really more like summers at sleep-away camp. At least the bad parts of camp. Like how we have to wake up early, follow a schedule, do stupid activities with the arts and crafts lady, and eat disgusting food you can name from its color. Everyone at camp knows that having "brown and yellow" for dinner means having meatloaf and mashed potatoes, except on days when they serve spaghetti and make the sauce really dark. The same thing happens here. Last night, I heard a nurse tell the man who wheels the trays around to give Nora "the brown one." It made me kind of homesick, just like at camp.

People also gossip like crazy at camp, but not as much as here. You wouldn't believe how gossipy sick kids can be. They always have to know what everyone's "in for." Basically, anything you get an IV for makes you more popular than just having a broken leg. But it's even better if you get to wear one of those oxygen masks, especially for little boys who pretend that they're famous astronauts about to go walking on the moon.

The funny thing is, though, it's not that easy being popular in the hospital. You have to be careful you don't look *too* sick, because once you have a bunch of machines hooked up to your body, it's not that neat anymore. It's kind of like how at camp, people are always making fun of the girls with either really small boobs or really humongous boobs, but the girls with the medium-sized boobs are pretty popular. In the hospital, if you have something small like a fever or something serious like leukemia, you can forget about people stopping by and saying how much they'll miss you when you leave.

The other thing about the hospital that's like camp is how everyone sizes up the new kids the minute they check in. It's kind of like you've formed a tent with your neighbors, and then whoever isn't stuck in bed goes to see what the new kid is like. The popular kids are the ones you hear talking on the phone to all their friends, and you can never see them behind all the helium balloons and flowers in their rooms. But the nerdy kids are the ones in the empty rooms, just lying there waiting for the phone to ring. They're always looking out into the hallway for someone to talk to, and they pretend they don't notice when the deliveryman keeps bringing stuffed animals for the popular kids in the other rooms. They're probably the kids who never get care packages at camp.

But the popular kids don't have it that bad here. If they

aren't too sick, most of them can get away with things when the nurses aren't looking. Like sneaking pretzels from the nurses lounge or going down the hall to visit kids in other rooms to see whose scar is grosser. It's just like sneaking around your counselor at camp.

For a while the hospital seems exactly like camp, except for one thing. One day you'll see an empty room that used to be the room with the cute baby in it, and you'll ask Elizabeth if you can switch rooms because that one has a color TV. You'll get all excited about switching rooms, but then you'll find out that the baby never went home. That's when you remember you're not at camp.

# Nora

"This isn't a game anymore," Dr. Katz said when he came in this morning. The reason he came early is that the treatment team is worried about my lab tests. Dr. Katz said he doesn't care what the chart says because I'm obviously not eating as much as the nurses are writing down, which is why he just had a talk with them about how they should never listen to me, no matter what. Like anyone ever listens to me anyway.

Then Dr. Katz started examining me, but I kept holding my breath because I didn't want to breathe in any calories from his breakfast. Every time he found something wrong, he'd say it out loud like there was another doctor in the room taking notes. "Acute dehydration," he said when he pulled at my skin. "Osteoporosis," he said when he looked at my X-rays. Then just when I forgot all about holding my breath, Dr. Katz sighed right into my face. It was pretty disgusting. Today his breath smelled like chewed-up sausage—210 calories per serving. I figured maybe about a third of it went up my nose, so I'd have to give up my slice of bread for lunch to make up for the 70 calories. But when I kept trying to cough the calories out, Dr. Katz said, "Suppressed immune functioning." I tried explaining that I was just coughing out the calories, but then he said I had "signs of dementia."

If you want my opinion, Dr. Katz was the one who was acting demented. Because all of a sudden he blurted out, "We won't let you die, darlin'!" like I was stuck in the bottom of a well or something. Then he said that if I don't eat, they'll have to stick a tube down my throat. I swear, that's what he said: *a tube!* I wondered if Dr. Katz would stick the tube down my throat himself since he loves sticking tongue depressors down kids' throats so much, or if maybe someone like Doug would do it. I definitely don't want Doug sticking a tube down my throat. I mean, he can't even rub pimple cream in.

I told Dr. Katz that I don't want The Tube, but he kept making it sound like all the doctors were more upset about it than me. "We're not happy about this at all," Dr. Katz said. "If you'd eat on your own, darlin', it would make things a lot easier on the team." Whoever *they* are.

That's why they're changing the 75% rule. The new rule is that I have to eat everything on my tray, even that piece of lettuce that's only there to decorate the plate. I told Dr. Katz that no one eats that piece of lettuce, and if I was in a restaurant and ate that piece of lettuce it would be considered bad etiquette. It's true, ask Mom. I also said that if I left that piece of lettuce on my plate in a restaurant, the chef wouldn't come running out of the kitchen and stick a tube down my throat because of it. But Dr. Katz just said the rules are different here, so I better clean my tray.


After Dr. Katz left, I started getting nervous about The Tube, so I tried calling Mom. I knew if Mom thought I might get a permanent scar on my neck, she'd call the doctors right away and complain. But when I picked up the phone, I heard Brownie's voice saying "Yes?" on the other end. I wondered if maybe I really did have dementia like Dr. Katz said, so I kept hanging up and picking up the phone again to see if Brownie's voice would go away. I was still picking up the phone and trying to get a dial tone when Brownie walked into my room.

"What do you need, child?" she asked. I could tell Brownie was still mad at me for being on a diet instead of having diabetes. "I'm trying to call my mom," I answered, "but something's wrong with my phone." Brownie didn't seem too worried about the phone being broken, though. She just walked over to the farthest corner of my room where I put the candy bird, grabbed a bunch of candies, and said, "Didn't Dr. Katz tell you? You can't use the phone no more until you eat." I couldn't believe they wouldn't let me call my own *mom*.

I didn't want to cry in front of Brownie because it would have made her too happy. Believe me, people who hate you love to see you cry. I wondered if Brownie would also be happy if they stuck The Tube down my throat, but then I figured out that Brownie's probably part of the treatment team Dr. Katz keeps talking about. It was probably her idea to take the phone away, and it was probably her idea to stick The Tube down my throat. I kept trying not to cry, but when I couldn't help it any more, I looked down at my book. A tear fell right on the part where Emma—that's Madame Bovary's first name—takes poison so she can get away from all the people who don't understand her. She spent the whole book trying to find someone who did, but she never could, so she had to drink the poison.

"Come on now, it's not all that bad, you know," Brownie said. "There's plenty do to without a telephone." Not when you're trapped in a hospital room and you can't even call your own mom, I was thinking, but I didn't feel like talking to Brownie. You can't trust anyone here, *especially* if they're on your treatment team.

•  •  •

After Brownie left, I decided to exercise. I was down on the floor doing leg-lifts on the far side of my bed where no one would see, when Brownie's white nurse's shoes showed up in front of my face again. "So you found something to do," she said. I practically had to turn my whole neck around to see Brownie's face, it was so high up, but I still couldn't see it because she was holding a stack of letters that got in the way. "These are all for you," she said, "and if you get up off the floor right now, I won't tell nobody what I saw."

I still had one more set of leg-lifts to do, but I was pretty curious about the letters and I didn't want to get The Tube stuck down my throat, so I got up and sat on a chair. I didn't tell Brownie, but my bones hurt from sitting, and I was feeling really dizzy. I was thirsty, too. They won't let me have water or Tab because everything I drink has to have calories, so I never drink anything here. Dr. Katz keeps saying I'm dehydrated, but if you want my opinion, it's his own fault for not giving me any water.

I tried forgetting about being dizzy when I looked at the mail. I was excited about getting such a big stack of letters, but then I realized what it was. It was a bunch of get-well letters from every kid in my grade. Mr. Miller must have made everyone write them, just like he does with the Valentine's Day cards. At first I was planning on throwing all the letters out, but to tell you the truth, I was kind of curious to see how phony Leslie's letter would be. I figured the one with all the exclamation marks on it would be hers since she's always writing notes like that in class. The envelope was hard to open, though, maybe because she put water on it instead of licking it closed. When I was still friends with Leslie and gave her a diet plan, I told her never to lick stamps or envelopes, no matter what. Here's what she wrote:

Hi Lori!!!!
Get well soon! We all miss you so much!!!!! I'd tell you every-

thing that's going on, but I'm writing notes with Chris right
now, so I don't have time! Get well sooooooon!!!!!!!!
Lots of hugs!! Leslie!

Gross. The only other letter I really wanted to read was the
one from Chris, but I didn't recognize his writing from the outside, so I had to open a lot of other envelopes before I found his.
All he wrote was, "Get well soon. You're really lucky that you
can eat as much junk food as you want. Sincerely, Chris." I
guess he was so busy passing notes to Leslie that he didn't have
time to write anything nice. I hate Mr. Miller for making everyone write to me. It's so embarrassing.

Mr. Miller also wrote me a letter, naturally. It said that
everyone misses me, and that all the teachers think I'm an absolute delight and can't wait for me to get better and come back
to school. Which is baloney, because Mrs. Rivers is probably
*thrilled* that I'm gone. I'll bet she threw a big party.

I was wondering if the reason Miss Shaw didn't write is because she's still mad about what I said about her boyfriend, but
then I smelled the lunch trays from the hallway. That meant it
was 11:00 on the dot. They're very strict here about serving
meals at exactly 6:30, 11:00, and 4:30. Brownie said it's "hospital policy. No exceptions," but normal people don't eat dinner
at 4:30. I mean, I'm usually just getting home from typing at
4:30. Everyone's telling me to try to be normal, but trust me,
no one's normal in this hospital.

That's why yesterday, when I couldn't stand getting woken
up for breakfast and eating dinner in the middle of the day, I
decided to reset the clock in my room to Washington, D.C.,
time because it's three hours later there. I figured I'd trick myself into thinking it was 9:30, 2:00, and 7:30 when my meals
came. It worked okay the first day, but then I heard Doug tell
Dr. Gold that he thought I was becoming "delusional." They
even started talking about giving me medicine, which probably
has a lot of calories. After that, I switched my clock back. It

would have been too much of a hassle trying to explain anything to them.

So lunch came exactly at 11:00, but on today's tray there was something new. It was this giant chocolate chip cookie wrapped in plastic that had huge colored letters spelling out MONSTER COOKIE! Putting this on the tray of someone on a diet is kind of like mailing a package to Superman with huge pictures of kryptonite on the outside. He'd obviously never open it, and neither did I. But I was still thinking about how Dr. Katz said I have to clean all the food off my tray, and I wasn't about to let anyone put The Tube down my throat because of a giant chocolate chip cookie. That's why I decided to go meet Nora. They didn't have enough nurses to watch me eat today, so I figured I'd hide my lunch in her room.

I waited until the coast was clear, then I went out into the hallway with my lunch stuffed under my sweatshirt. It was weird seeing Nora's room. It already looked like a regular teenager's room, even though she just got here. The walls were covered with Bee Gee posters, and she had about a million different perfume bottles and lipsticks on her nightstand. I'll bet Mom would love Nora. Nora also had so many shoes they didn't fit into the closet, and on the table next to her bed, she had a pink radio with heart-shaped stickers all over it. The radio was on when I got there.

I couldn't see Nora's face at first because she was lying under a bunch of magazines. So I walked up to her bed, and that's when I noticed she was sleeping. I'll admit this is a nosy thing to do, but I heard that Nora's popular at school and I was curious to see what the popular girls in high school keep in their rooms. So I opened the drawer next to her bed, but the noise started waking Nora up. I couldn't wait to get out of there, which is probably why I tripped over the cord to her radio on the way out.

The music stopped, and then the machines she was hooked up to started beeping all of a sudden. I didn't notice the machines before because Nora had them covered with these pink, lacy sheets. The machines kept beeping and Nora looked right at me, but I didn't know what to do. If I got caught, I figured I'd get punished with The Tube, but I couldn't just leave since Nora didn't seem like she could breathe. She was making a weird noise. That's when all the nurses came running in. Luckily, they were so busy fixing the beeping machines that they didn't even notice me. So I sneaked back to my room, jumped on my bed, turned on the TV, grabbed some books, and tried to look like I'd been in there for hours. But I still couldn't calm down, because I thought maybe I killed Nora by accident. Then I heard one of the nurses ask Nora what happened, and I knew for sure I'd get The Tube.

Nora was alive, thank God, but instead of telling on me, she said she had no idea how the radio fell, and she didn't say a word about me barging in. "I must have been kicking around in my sleep," she told them, but she didn't sound like she was lying or anything. Nora has one of those really innocent voices that adults always believe, even when you're totally lying. I kind of liked Nora.

The thing is, I still had to get rid of all the food from my tray before Brownie came in to write down how much I ate. I was thinking about flushing the food down the toilet, but it got kind of clogged from the pancakes and maple syrup I flushed down this morning, so I figured I'd go find a trash can out in the hallway instead. But when I was walking past Nora's room with the Monster Cookie, the turkey sandwich, and even that stupid piece of decoration lettuce hidden under my sweatshirt, Nora took off her oxygen mask and called me over. I thought she'd start telling me how horrible I am, like everyone else does, but she was more interested in finding out why I'm here.

I sat on Nora's couch and told her about The Tube and how I

wanted to hide my turkey sandwich and Monster Cookie in her room so the nurses would think I ate lunch. She said she couldn't understand why I think I'm fat, but because Bonnie won't let Nora eat any good food, Nora took my sandwich and stuffed the meat into her mouth in about thirty seconds. Then she did the same thing with my Monster Cookie. I kept staring at Nora and waiting for her to blow up like one of those Ball Park franks, but nothing happened. Nora's body didn't blow up, even though she ate so many calories. Trust me, my body would have.

Nora was so excited about getting to eat my lunch that she said I could bring her all my meals, especially the Monster Cookies. "If you stay here long enough," she said, "you'll learn to break a lot of rules." I asked Nora how long she's been here, and she told me that number 4002 is "her" room since she comes here every few weeks for her cystic fibrosis. She didn't make it sound very serious, but then she said that if she dies here, she wants it to be in a room just like hers at home. "Do you think you'll die?" I asked, but Nora didn't answer. She looked like she might start crying, but instead she asked if I wanted to borrow her new *Teen* magazine, or the one with Andy Gibb on the cover.

I took the magazine with Andy Gibb since my favorite song is "I Just Want to Be Your Everything," and Nora looked away and started reading *Teen.* But I didn't go right to the Andy Gibb article because I kept looking at this Maybelline ad that showed a picture of a skinny girl with beautiful skin and a great smile. She looked just like Nora. I kept thinking how if I saw Nora at school, she'd probably be one of those snobby girls who always wear lip gloss and blush and look like the girl in the Maybelline ad. I'll bet she wouldn't even *talk* to me outside the hospital. But then I kind of wondered what would happen if I actually knew any of those girls the way I know Nora. Because maybe if their makeup smeared off, there'd be tons of pimples underneath. And maybe the popular girls' pimples would be these disgusting blackheads ten times bigger than my pimples ever are.

# Hey, Taxi

Even though I wasn't allowed to look at the scale, when Elizabeth woke me up to weigh me, I could tell that I lost more weight. She said if I don't eat all my meals today, the doctors will definitely put me on hyperalimentation. That's the real name for The Tube. When breakfast came, Elizabeth sat with me while I ate a few bites of a banana and Special K, but the minute I stopped eating, Elizabeth asked if I was done. I said I was, and Elizabeth answered, "If you were my daughter, I'd tell them to put you on hyperal right away."

I told Elizabeth that she must not love her daughter very much, but Elizabeth said she loves her very much and that's *why* she'd let the doctors put The Tube down her throat. Then I asked if she knew when her daughter was born that she'd have to chauffeur her around to math enrichment and doctors' appointments, but Elizabeth didn't answer. She just said that even though she's not very good at math, at least she knows 100% means the entire meal. I saw her write down that I ate 0%. I tried explaining that I ate at least 5%, but Elizabeth wrote down 0% anyway. "I know you don't like this," she said, "but it's for your own good." I couldn't believe she'd turn against me, too. I figured I'd *definitely* be getting The Tube.

• • •

That's why the second Elizabeth left, I decided to sneak into Nora's room to see if I could use her phone to call Mom. I knew I had to do something about The Tube before it was too late. Nora was sitting up in bed today, and she was putting on blush in a tiny mirror that came with her makeup kit. You could tell she knows exactly how to do it so it follows her cheekbones. Once when I tried putting on blush, I couldn't find the bone that Mom's *Redbook* said to follow. I think I'm missing that bone because I can see a lot of bones in my face, but I still can't find the right one.

Anyway, Nora wouldn't stop staring at herself. She was still looking in her tiny mirror when she asked if I had any more Monster Cookies to give her. I told her I wouldn't get one until the lunches came. So Nora said to be sure to remember to bring her the cookie later, but I told her I'd only bring it if she'd let me use her phone to call my mom. Nora said okay, but then her phone rang and I had to wait.

I could tell it was Nora's mom on the phone, and they wouldn't stop talking. So I sat on the couch and looked through some magazines, because I was scared that if I left, Nora might not let me use the phone when I came back. I was reading the Andy Gibb article so I could learn about how he comes up with the ideas for his songs, when all of a sudden Nora screamed so loud I practically jumped off the couch. Which proves Dr. Katz is wrong about my reflexes not working anymore.

Nora screamed because her mom told her that the doctors are letting her go back home tomorrow morning. I know I was sup- posed to be happy for Nora, but I couldn't help wondering what I'll do with my Monster Cookies if she goes home. Besides, I kind of want someone nice to be here with me if I get The Tube. I guess I want someone to hold my hand the way I hold Mom's hand when she gets scared at Dr. Katz's office. Now I'll be all alone.

When Nora finally hung up, she handed me the phone, but I didn't call my mom. I was planning on calling her, but then I changed my mind and called Jaclyn Smith. I was hoping that she and the Angels might come over right away and help me escape, but the lady who answered said she wouldn't be home until after dinner. I obviously couldn't wait that long, so next I dialed information, then I called the number the information lady gave me for the taxi company. "I'd like a cab, please," I said, and the man asked me where from and where to. I gave him my address, and he said that a cab would be out front in fifteen minutes.

I made Nora swear she wouldn't tell the nurses where I went, but Nora said she already lied for me yesterday, and that even though she breaks the rules, she didn't think I should be leaving the hospital. She obviously didn't understand about The Tube. So I told her that if she lied for me just this one last time, I'd promise to send her an entire box of Monster Cookies every week for the next month, and she agreed right away.

I only had fifteen minutes, so I went to my room and packed a few things into my backpack. I packed all my diet books, my chess set, a picture of my bird, Chrissy, and a softball so I'd have something to play with in case Maria was out at the market and I couldn't get in the house for a while. My sweatpants wouldn't fit in my backpack, but I figured since Mom loves going shopping so much, she'd probably buy me new ones the second I got home anyway. Then I took off the only piece of jewelry I ever wear, my gold necklace, and put it in my pocket. That's what I was planning on using to pay for the cab ride.

Nora was great at going along with our plan. She called all the nurses into her room while I sneaked by and started walking toward the elevators. Then I walked right past the receptionist, but when I was waiting for the elevator, Doug and Mike came out of another elevator that was going up. I thought they might catch me, but they were too busy wheeling a kid hooked up to a bunch of tubes back toward the ward. I figured I'd look exactly like that if they gave me The Tube, so I was really glad I was leaving the hospital.

When I got downstairs, there were a lot of taxicabs picking people up and dropping them off. I had no idea which was mine, so I went up to the only empty one and asked the driver if he was looking for me. "Sure, get in," the driver said, except he didn't start the motor or anything.

The thing is, I didn't have a lot of time because even Nora couldn't kiss up to the nurses forever, so finally I told the driver that we should get going, but he wouldn't budge. He just kept looking at me in his rearview mirror. "Where's your mom?" he asked, and I told him that she was probably out shopping, but I didn't have time to talk right now. Then the driver asked, "Where's your pop?" I figured he really wanted to have a conversation, because driving a cab must be a very lonely job. "My dad's at work," I said. "But he'll be home after the stock market closes in New York." The driver still didn't pull away, though. He just tossed his cigarette out the window and lit up another one while I tried not to breathe too much.

Then all of a sudden the driver turned his neck around and glared at me in the backseat. He told me he thought I was with my mom or my pop and he couldn't take a kid away from the hospital like this. He pointed at my hospital ID bracelet and said I was obviously not supposed to be leaving the hospital, and that he would lose his job if he drove me home. The reason he couldn't lose his job is because he had two kids at home to feed, not to mention his wife. I told the driver that if he didn't take me home I'd get a gigantic tube stuck down my throat, but he just said he had his own kids' problems to worry about, and that I had to get out of his cab because he was losing fares by spending all his time arguing with me.

That's when I took the gold necklace out of my pocket. I tried to convince the driver that the necklace would be worth more than the fares he'd get if he didn't drive me home. So he put his cigarette down in the ashtray and stared at the gold chain. I kept dangling the necklace in front of his eyes like I've seen those hypnotists do on TV, and for a second the driver looked like he might be going into a real trance. But then another cab honked at us, which ruined the mood. That's when the driver said if I didn't get out of his cab, he'd use his CB to tell "the authorities" that I was running away. I guess he meant the police, or maybe my treatment team.

I obviously didn't have much of a choice, so I put the gold necklace back in my pocket and got out of the cab. But the driver didn't wait for another fare like he said he would. He sped off the second I slammed the door closed. Then I sat down on the steps and slid the stupid ID bracelet off my wrist so the next cab driver wouldn't kick me out. I was surprised that the bracelet came off my wrist so fast, because I couldn't get it off the last time I tried.

I figured I'd find another driver who'd want the necklace, so I got up and waited on the sidewalk again. But I felt dizzy when I stood up, like I might faint. I kept thinking about how it would be a terrible time to faint, but then I sat down on the steps again and I felt a little better. I waited a long time before I saw another empty taxicab. The minute I saw one, I jumped up to grab it before anyone else did, but I got so dizzy I had to sit down right away, and someone else took it. To tell you the truth, I was getting kind of scared. I would have been fine if Dr. Katz ever let me drink some water. Plus it was really sunny out where I was sitting and it hurt my eyes to look out for cabs. Then it hurt my eyes just to be opened. I also had a terrible headache again, even worse than the one my parents gave me on the way to the hospital. It was the worst headache I've ever had, so I decided I'd go back into the hospital to a different ward and ask for some aspirin and water. Then I'd be able to jump up quick enough to grab an empty cab before anyone else could.

I practically fainted when I stood up again, but I figured by this time the nurses were probably running around the halls looking for me, so I kept going anyway. I didn't want anyone calling my parents because I didn't want them getting mad at me before I got home and had a chance to explain about The Tube and why I had to run away. I mean, my parents don't listen anyway, but they're even worse listeners when they're *already* mad about something. So I went back in, but a security guard grabbed me by my shoulders and used his walkie-talkie to tell someone they found me. I tried to get away from the man but he was pretty big and I felt too dizzy to move. I'm not sure if I actually fainted, but the next thing I knew I was sitting on the guard's feet.


I'm pretty tired right now, so I don't feel like going into everything that happened when they took me back upstairs. Except for the part when Dr. Gold told me that Nora told the nurses where I went because she was worried about me. Dr. Gold said everyone's worried about me, and he hopes that now I realize how many people care about me. I told Dr. Gold that if so many people cared they wouldn't put a big tube down my throat, but Dr. Gold said that putting a tube in is a sign of caring. "Oh, yeah? Have you ever seen a Hallmark card with pictures of people sticking tubes down each other's throats?" I asked, but Dr. Gold just sat there and nodded even longer than usual.

Finally Dr. Gold said that he'll talk to Dr. Katz so I can get a few more days to gain weight before they make me get The Tube. He also said I can use the phone and see my parents, because if I'm not so lonely here, maybe I'll feel like eating. Plus I get to eat meals at normal times now, and no one has to sit with me. I figured there'd be a catch, though, and that's when Dr. Gold said that from now on, I'll be on something called "twenty-four-hour watch." I didn't know what that was supposed to mean, but Dr. Gold said it means I'll get caught right away if I ever leave my room again. He didn't say exactly what would happen if I got caught, but whatever it is, I'm sure it has something to do with making my life more miserable. If that's even possible.

# Shereen's Jeans

There's a catch to everything in this hospital. I finally got to sleep late, but the second I woke up, Bonnie came in. She said that Dr. Gold wants me to fill out meal cards again, except this time we have to do them together. "It'll be fun!" she said in her excited voice. Real fun. Bonnie wanted me to request fattening things like omelets and sausage, but I told her that normal women don't eat that much food at breakfast. The Special K lady doesn't. Bonnie kept saying they do, though, so I told her that if she would eat the exact breakfast she puts on my tray each morning, in front of me, I'd think about eating it, too. That's when Bonnie said she'd tell Dr. Gold how uncooperative I am, and I said I'd tell Dr. Gold what a phony she is.

Before my 4:00 session with Dr. Gold, I heard Bonnie complaining about how I want her to eat the huge breakfast with me, but Dr. Gold thought it would be a good idea. Then Bonnie said that she only eats a piece of toast for breakfast, so Dr. Gold asked if Bonnie could eat lunch with me instead. He called it "modeling" and thought it would be good for me to see adults eating healthy-sized meals. Bonnie sure didn't like that idea. "I give her a 400-calorie chocolate chip cookie on her lunch tray," she practically yelled. "I can't eat that! Besides, I spend my lunch hour exercising." Some nutritionist.

When Dr. Gold came into my room, I asked him why they weren't putting The Tube down Bonnie's throat because of how little she eats. But Dr. Gold said that one of my problems is that I worry too much about what everyone else is doing when I should be focusing on myself. That's why he's decided to film me. It's this new plan he has so I won't have to get The Tube. Dr. Gold wants me to take a good look at myself instead of worrying about what everyone else sees. I told Dr. Gold that I already spend hours looking at myself, which is why I know I'm fat, but he said he feels I'll see myself better in a film.

Dr. Gold explained that they'll film me tomorrow, but they'll be careful to block out my face so I can be used as a "case study" for other doctors to watch. Then he said that I'm an "excellent case," which is why they picked me in the first place. I guess that means I'm an excellent dieter. I was thinking about how it means I'm the best dieter at my school, and I'm probably the best dieter in the country, maybe even the world! I mean, I must be, because they want to make a *movie* of me. I was pretty excited about it, but then I thought that maybe the doctors watching my film would have seen thinner anorexics than me. That's because I remembered the pictures Dr. Katz showed me before I came to the hospital.

The last time I went to Dr. Katz's office, he showed me pictures of all these bony-looking women that had the words, "Anorexic, Female" written underneath. The reason they had to write the word "female" is because these women didn't look much like women. They looked more like the big skeleton that hangs in the corner of our science classroom, and I have no idea if that skeleton is supposed to be a man or a woman. I always thought there was something wrong with it, because whoever made it put two bones connecting each ankle to each knee, and I was almost positive there was only one bone going between your ankle and your knee. I figured the school bought a broken skeleton on sale or something because they're always telling us not to waste our supplies.

In the pictures in Dr. Katz's book, though, I saw that humans really *do* have two bones right next to each other between the ankle and the knee. I guess Dr. Katz figured that the pictures would scare me into eating, because he kept looking at my face to see if I was getting grossed out. But when I told him how neat it was that humans actually do have two separate bones in the bottoms of our legs, even though it looks like only one, he just blew all this air out of his mouth and said my brain wasn't working right because I'm so malnourished. The truth is, my brain wasn't working right because of his smelly breath.

Anyway, that's why I figured Dr. Gold made a big mistake calling me an "excellent case." I mean, if *that's* what a real anorexic looks like, I'd be a pretty bad example. So I decided not to eat anything until after the filming tomorrow. Not one bite.


After Dr. Gold left, I was climbing up on the couch to try to look at myself in the window when I noticed Mom standing in my doorway with a bright red Saks shopping bag. So I climbed down and she came in my room, closed the door, and handed me the bag. I knew right away that she brought my friend Shereen's jeans. Actually, my ex-friend Shereen. Shereen's mom and my mom were pregnant with us at the same time, so we've been friends for life. Except something happened this year. Shereen's mom is French, and all of a sudden Shereen started getting huge French boobs like her mom's. That's when Shereen became one of the popular girls. I haven't really talked to her much lately, but Mom gets a big kick out of talking about what a beautiful body Shereen has. She's always asking why I can't look like Shereen.

Last night on the phone, Mom asked me again why I can't look like Shereen. I told her that I can't look like Shereen because even with those heavy boobs, Shereen weighs less than me. But right after I said it, I knew exactly what Mom was planning on saying, and when she said, "You don't weigh anything anymore," I kind of mouthed it along with her, even though she couldn't see me through the phone. "Well, you don't," Mom said, like she really *could* see me. We have this conversation all the time. I swear, we could go on for years with me saying, "I do, too," and Mom saying, "Oh, please, don't you ever look at yourself in the mirror?" and me thinking, "I would if the doctors would give me one." That's why I blurted out, "Bring me a pair of Shereen's jeans, and I'll show you that Shereen's much thinner than me."

So today Mom brought the jeans to the hospital. She was sitting on the couch and I was about to take off my baggy sweats, when all of a sudden Doug walked in. He said that I needed to drink some orange juice because I'm so dizzy. I told him if he brought me some water I'd drink that, but Doug said the whole point of drinking the orange juice was to raise my blood sugar level.

I tried telling Doug that nothing was wrong with my blood sugar level, but the truth is, I *was* feeling dizzy again. So I took exactly one sip of the orange juice. Then Doug said I had to drink five more sips, but when I wouldn't he didn't get mad because he was too busy talking to Mom about some girl she wants to set him up with. She's twenty-two and she's trying to be an actress. Mom thinks she's "absolutely adorable" and has "a fabulous figure." Doug said he doesn't have much time to get out and meet people, so Mom took her address book out of her big purse and wrote down the girl's number for Doug. Then Doug left and luckily he forgot about making me drink the orange juice.

After that, I started putting on the jeans. I was positive I was right about Shereen being thinner than me. I figured she weighs at least ten pounds less. So I held in my stomach and pulled the jeans up past my thighs, even though I was sure I wouldn't be able to button them at my waist. But when I closed the last button, I saw Mom staring at me. Except she didn't say anything like, "Why can't you look like Shereen?" this time. Instead she looked down at the floor.

I was happy about the jeans buttoning, but then I looked to where Mom was looking, and that's when I saw the jeans all scrunched up on my feet. Which made no sense. I mean, I'm so much fatter than Shereen. I wondered if the jeans Mom brought were really Shereen's, or if they were really some fat girl's jeans used to trick me, like those trick birthday candles that don't go out, no matter how hard you blow. I wanted the real jeans, not the trick ones.

I didn't know why the jeans fell off, but I was pretty sure I was still right about Shereen being thinner than me. I told Mom that since Shereen is two inches taller than me, that's why the jeans were too big. "Oh, please," Mom answered, so I gave her more reasons why the jeans didn't fit. I even said that Shereen's mom uses this laundry detergent that stretches all their clothes out, but then Mom stopped saying "Oh, please" for once. She just kept staring at the jeans on the floor. Then she got up and said that Dad would be coming by after his tennis game to see me. I really wanted to try the jeans on again, but Mom put them back in the Saks bag and took them home.


After Mom left, I kept thinking about Shereen's jeans. I was sort of wondering if it's even possible for me to be skinnier than Shereen. It was finally dark out, so I stood up on the couch and looked in the glass window to check. I could see my collarbone and my ribs, but my stomach still looked fat. Then I checked my butt, which was also fat, and my thighs, which looked okay from the side, and made sure my kneecaps still stuck out. That's when I looked below my knees, and this time I actually saw those two separate bones in the bottom of each leg. I couldn't believe it!

I got a little scared when I touched those bones because I kept thinking about the gross pictures Dr. Katz showed me. So I got off the couch, since I didn't like looking at them anymore. But after a while I got curious again, so I climbed back up to look. And then I felt great, because I figured that Dr. Gold might be right about something for once in his life. I mean, maybe I really *am* an "excellent case."

# Life without Andy Gibb

Because it's Wednesday, Dr. Katz came to the hospital in his green golf clothes instead of his usual white coat. The first thing he said was that we needed to have a talk, but it turns out that Dr. Katz's idea of having a talk is for *him* to do all the talking. He said that Dr. Gold thinks it would be better if I know what my target weight is, because then I'll feel more in control. I wasn't really interested in knowing some weight I'm never planning on reaching, but it didn't matter because Dr. Katz wanted to tell me anyway. "Your target weight is . . . ," Dr. Katz said, but it took him a while to get it out, like he was announcing the winner of a big Academy Award or something, ". . . sixty pounds!"

I wish Dr. Katz never told me about my target weight. I'll never weigh 60 pounds, even if I have to live here for the rest of my life. So I couldn't wait for Dr. Gold to show up after that, because he was supposed to film me for the case study. I was still excited about it, and I only had one sip of orange juice since yesterday so I'd look like an excellent case. I mean, I didn't want to be a phony anorexic or anything. But Dr. Gold didn't bring a movie camera and bright lights like I expected.

He was only carrying his stupid notepad. He told me he decided not to do the case study with me because he felt I got too excited about it, and it would just make me feel good about being emaciated. "But I'm an excellent case!" I said, then Dr. Gold said this was exactly why he wouldn't film me. I'll bet the real reason is that I'm too fat after all.

I didn't see any sense in paying someone to make you even more miserable than you were in the first place, so I told Dr. Gold that he was a terrible psychiatrist and he was fired. But Dr. Gold didn't leave like he was supposed to. He just kept sitting on my couch and nodding. Finally I tried explaining that "fired" means you have to leave and not come back, but Dr. Gold still wouldn't budge.

"I know what 'fired' means," Dr. Gold whispered, "but I'm wondering what it means for you." Dr. Gold always asks *you* a question when he doesn't want to talk about something. It was such a stupid question I didn't bother answering. Then he started boring me with his favorite subject—control—so I flipped on the TV. That got Dr. Gold pretty excited. He said that turning on the TV was another "act of control" and it's great that I'm acting out my control on something besides food. But instead of leaving my room, he just sat there nodding again, like his neck was the only part of his body that could move.

Since Dr. Gold wouldn't go, I figured I'd leave instead. That's why all of a sudden I got up and walked down to this patio area where all the doctors who tell you not to smoke take their smoking breaks. None of the nurses even tried to stop me. So much for twenty-four-hour watch. Then I stayed down on the patio and sat on a bench next to a tree in a wooden planter. All the trees on the patio were in tiny planters, and you could tell the trees would break the planters if they grew any bigger.

The hospital probably had to keep the trees tiny so they'd look nice on the patio, but I felt bad because the hospital didn't give *them* any water either. The soil was totally dry.

I figured Dr. Gold was probably gone by then, but instead of going up to my room, I thought I might go downstairs and look for another taxicab. Not to go home, but maybe to a bus station so I could run away to a place where I wouldn't have to weigh 60 pounds. I decided not to, though, partly because I didn't have my gold necklace on, and partly because when I stood up, I remembered how dizzy I got the last time I went to look for a cab, and I was feeling dizzy again. I just wanted to go upstairs and go to sleep. I wanted to sleep so long that I'd never wake up. So I came back here, but none of the nurses noticed I was gone. Dr. Gold's not even here anymore. Obviously, no one cares.

I wish I could be like Emma in the part in *Madame Bovary* where she drinks the poison and goes to heaven. Except they never tell you in the book how Emma decided to go through with it. I wonder if she made a list, but I doubt it. She was probably too busy sneaking around and having affairs to sit down and make a list. I guess she just disappeared one day, and that was it.

Sometimes I feel like maybe I've disappeared, too, but I can't tell for sure. I guess the only way to know if you're still here is if you write things down. I mean, you know the *paper's* here.

REASONS WHY I SHOULDN'T KILL MYSELF:

1. Will miss Chrissy a lot
2. Will never get to meet Andy Gibb
3. Lots of big bugs underground
4. The phony funeral will make me puke, but I'll be dead anyway, so I probably won't notice

REASONS WHY I SHOULD KILL MYSELF:

1. Won't get The Tube
2. Won't have to be ladylike
3. Won't have to talk to Dr. Gold about control
4. Won't have to see Dad's vein pop out
5. Won't have to go shopping with Mom
6. No one makes you eat when you're dead
7. Won't have to be a secretary my whole life if I grow up fat
8. It's the only way to get out of the hospital without weighing 60 pounds

# Cutting the Fat

I guess it's a lot easier deciding to kill yourself than actually doing it. All kinds of things can go wrong, even if you think you know how. I mean, I knew about people hanging themselves or sitting in their cars and dying from the gas, but I couldn't do those things because I'm too short to tie something to the ceiling and I don't drive yet. Then I thought about drinking poison like Madame Bovary did, but I got scared that if it didn't work, I'd wake up fat from all the calories.

The only other way I knew to kill yourself was to use a razor blade and bleed to death. That way seemed okay because I'm pretty brave when Dr. Katz takes blood from me, but I didn't have a razor blade. So when I saw the paints and scissors the arts and crafts lady left for me, I figured I'd use the scissors instead. My plan was to pretend I was doing some kind of art project on my body, then it wouldn't hurt as much when I first started cutting. I was kind of scared about the cutting part, but not about the dying part. I couldn't wait to be dead.

So I picked up the scissors and closed my eyes, but then I didn't know where I was supposed to cut myself. I figured most of my blood was probably in my heart, but all of my ribs were in the way. I swear, I have like a thousand ribs. But then I felt my stomach, and I knew exactly where to cut. I wanted to cut all the fat off my body so people like Leslie wouldn't say I looked fat at my funeral. Knowing Mom, she'd probably dress me up in a mohair sweater and leave the coffin open. So I put the tip of the scissors right under my belly button where if I pulled really hard, I could pinch an inch. Well, if I weighed 60 pounds, I'll bet I could.

Since the scissors felt pretty cold, I held them against my stomach for a minute to warm them up, but they stayed cold anyway because my body's always cold lately. I wanted to cut myself fast, like when you rip off a Band-Aid, so I closed my eyes again, but I could hear my heart beating like mad. It was really pounding, which I thought was good because that meant a lot of blood was flowing through all my veins. That's when I cut into my stomach, but I didn't get very far because Elizabeth walked in with my dinner tray. Then the tray fell on the floor.

I don't remember exactly what happened after that, because I got dizzy again. I don't even remember if it hurt when I cut into the fat. All I remember is lying on the bed with the door closed and seeing Elizabeth sitting on the couch in the dark. At first I thought I might be in heaven, so right away I felt my stomach to see if heaven made me thin, but all I felt were a bunch of Band-Aids. That's when I knew I was still fat and still in the hospital, and that Elizabeth put the Band-Aids on my stomach to keep me from bleeding.

"I'm gonna get The Tube now, aren't I?" I asked Elizabeth. Elizabeth said she didn't know, but that I should just go back to sleep for now. She said she didn't tell anyone yet about what she saw, so I could have some time to rest before people came in and started bugging me. She thought everyone would make a big deal out of what I did, and even though it *was* a very big deal, they'd probably all argue in front of me about what to do, and that would just make me want to do it over. Then Elizabeth said that no one knows what to do with me.

"I really don't care what people do with me," I told her. "I really don't care about anything anymore." I meant it, too.

"Well I do," Elizabeth said. "I care a lot."

I opened my eyes to see if I was dreaming, but I wasn't because I saw Elizabeth sitting on the couch by the window in her white nurse's outfit. She looked like an angel, then for a second she looked like the big white polar bear we saw at the zoo. But mostly like an angel with a nurse's name tag. That's all I remember before I fell asleep.

# Secretary School

"Why did you do it?" Elizabeth asked when I woke up. I couldn't tell if she wanted to know why I was cutting the fat off my stomach, or why I wanted to die. So I told her that I wanted to die because I don't want to be fat, but Dr. Katz says I have to weigh 60 pounds. And even though I kind of *want* to stop dieting, I can't because then I might have to go to secretary school.

"Secretary school?" Elizabeth asked. I tried explaining how people say that fat girls have to go to secretary school until they get thin enough to find a husband, and how even though I like typing a lot, I know I'd get incredibly bored typing someone else's letters all day. I'd rather be dead. I'd also rather be dead than worry about being skinny all the time, but if you *don't* worry about being thin, everyone thinks you're a complete weirdo. Then Elizabeth said that she's not worried about being skinny and she's a nurse. Plus she has a husband and a five-year-old daughter. I was kind of curious about her daughter.

"What do you want to know about her?" Elizabeth asked. I told her that I was curious about what it was like when she was actually having her baby. I wondered if it was always terrible having babies, because then it wouldn't be that bad if I ever get fat and have to be alone for the rest of my life. But Elizabeth said having a baby isn't terrible at all. She even said she feels sorry for her husband because he'll never be able to get pregnant and give birth. "And it doesn't take very long to lose the weight afterward, if that's what you're worried about," she said, but I told her I was much more interested in the childbirth part than the weight part, for once.

Unlike Mom, Elizabeth really liked childbirth. "It was wonderful," she said, "but more than wonderful. It was beautiful, actually, but more than beautiful. It was . . ." She wasn't any better at English than she was at math, so I figured I should help her out. "Supernatural?" I asked. "Yes! Supernatural!" Elizabeth shouted. Then she told me she'd bring in some pictures from when she had her baby, but I told her that I already saw a movie in school about childbirth and my mom told me about it, too. That's when Elizabeth said that my mom was really lucky to have a daughter like me, and that if the doctors had put a baby like me in Elizabeth's arms when she was in the hospital, she would have thought it was a supernatural day.

I knew that Elizabeth's shift already ended, but the truth is, I was scared about what happened. I was sort of scared about everything that's happened—going on a diet, ending up in a hospital, cutting myself. I really liked having Elizabeth around, but the only thing I could think of to say was, "Your daughter must think you're supernatural, too." That made Elizabeth's eyes tear up, and I was embarrassed for saying something so sappy, so I turned on the TV. We made fun of all the ladies on commercials who got incredibly excited about mopping the floor or cleaning the kitchen counter, and Elizabeth promised that I'd never end up like them. She said if I did, then I could kill myself, but she was positive I'd have a much more exciting life. She told me I had a lot going for me, and I shouldn't waste it on a stupid diet.

Finally Elizabeth said she had to report that I cut myself.

"Promise never to try it again. Ever. Will you promise?" she asked. She was looking me right in the eye, and I couldn't believe she trusted my promises. Everyone else thinks I'm a liar, and I have to admit, I've been lying a lot since I started dieting. So I didn't answer, partly because I thought I might be lying, and partly because Elizabeth started talking again. "You won't have to be a secretary, you know. I can promise you that." I don't know why, but I really believed Elizabeth's promise. So finally I said that I promised, too. Then Elizabeth told me to remember that I'm much more interesting than people who worry about their weight all their lives, and that she'd come back and talk some more first thing in the morning. On the way out, she took my arts and crafts supplies with her.

After Elizabeth left, I was still thinking about the day I was born, when all of a sudden I remembered that today's my half birthday. It's the first day of summer, and I'm exactly eleven and a half. I usually make a wish on my half birthdays, so I was thinking that I'd wish to be the thinnest girl at school, or maybe even the thinnest eleven-year-old on the entire planet. Then I'd never have to worry about dieting anymore. I was just about to make the wish, but I sort of wondered what I'll have left to wish for on my real birthday, if I finally get that thin. I mean, what are girls supposed to wish for, other than being thin?

I didn't know what to wish for, because even if you *are* thin, you still have to worry that you won't get fat. Plus you're dizzy and tired all the time, but even then you can't eat because you start hating yourself for eating *anything*. You feel like you'll be fat no matter what. I sort of wished that I could just eat how I used to, like David and Dad do. I wished that I didn't have to feel hungry all the time, or care about people thinking I'm skinny enough. I wished being thin didn't matter so much to everyone, even *me*. So that's what I ended up wishing for.

# North Star

Dr. Katz had a huge smile on his face when he came to see me today. He said the whole treatment team is thrilled that I ate part of my breakfast and lunch because if I keep eating, they won't have to give me The Tube. "You know, darlin'," he said, "as much you've complained about Dr. Gold, he sure is helping you to see how skinny you are." Baloney. I told Dr. Katz that I probably got fat from all that milk I drank, but from now on I'm not listening to people who say you have to diet your whole life. It has nothing to do with Dr. Gold. But Dr. Katz said that Dr. Gold would be coming in anyway to talk to me about "that cutting business," like I opened up a knife store or something.

When Dr. Gold showed up, I told him that I'm not on a diet anymore, so his work is done. But Dr. Gold didn't believe me. He said he felt I was probably just eating so I wouldn't get The Tube, and he wants me to "resolve my issues" before I leave the hospital. In the meantime, though, I'll get a bunch of new privileges. I asked if my first new privilege could be to get rid of him once and for all, but Dr. Gold said I also have to learn how to talk nicely to people before I leave, and I told him that he has to learn how to talk to people in the first place instead of nodding all the time.

Then I played chess with myself on my bed while Dr. Gold sat on the couch and nodded. Every once in a while he'd ask me what I was feeling, and when I wouldn't answer, he'd whisper something about control that would make me lose my concentration. I finally figured out that if you don't answer Dr. Gold right away when he asks how you feel, he'll go ahead and give you the answer. So when I didn't say anything, Dr. Gold explained that I was feeling hostile, and that's why I cut myself yesterday.

I was hoping Dr. Gold would be quiet so I could play chess, but instead he started asking me about control again. So to make him happy, I told Dr. Gold that cutting myself made me feel more in control. I thought that would definitely shut him up, but he said my answer was wrong. He said that control has to do with *eating,* and hostility has to do with *cutting.* I swear, talking to Dr. Gold is sort of like taking one of those bubble tests in school where there's only one right answer to each question. It's a lot easier letting him tell you what you're feeling instead of trying to guess the answer and getting it wrong all the time.

After Dr. Gold left, Bonnie tapped on my door and walked in. She always knocks but then walks right in anyway. Bonnie's smile was even bigger than Dr. Katz's, and the first thing she said was how happy she is I started eating, even though it's not nearly enough to make me healthy again. One thing you should know about Bonnie is that she always has to say a bad thing right after a good thing. Like she'll say, "Vitamin A is good for your eyes, but it'll make your skin turn orange." Today Bonnie said it's great that I'm eating, but I have a very long way to go. Then she said that I can choose anything I want on the menu cards, but it might be hard to get things that taste good because it's still hospital food. Before she left, she said to keep up the good work, but to remember that my stomach will look fat at first because it needs to stretch itself out. Then she gave me my meal cards, and she drew a happy face on each one. I never got any happy faces on my meal cards before I started eating. Yesterday I was "uncooperative," but today everyone likes me all of a sudden, like I'm a completely different person because I ate half a turkey sandwich.

I guess I fell asleep after doing the meal cards, because Elizabeth woke me up for dinner. But she said she didn't have to sit with me while I ate because that was also one of my new privileges. I wanted her to stay anyway, though, so I asked her what it's like being a nurse. I've been thinking about what else I might want to be if I'm not a secretary. Elizabeth said that nurses watch patients and do whatever the doctors order. Plus you have to change people's bedpans. What a terrible job. I decided against that, obviously, but Elizabeth said she does it because she likes helping people.

"I don't need help," I told Elizabeth, but she changed the subject and asked what I want to be if I'm not a nurse. I never really thought about it before. I mean, my friends' moms spend all day dieting and shopping. I just know what I *don't* want do. So Elizabeth asked what I like, and I tried explaining how I once read a book on astrophysics, which sounded pretty interesting. That, or being a dancer, because I really liked the dance we learned to the music from *Welcome Back, Kotter* for the talent show.

Then Elizabeth did the funniest thing. She started waltzing with me around the room. That wasn't the kind of dancing I was talking about, but we ended up by the window and I showed her the constellations that I learned about from the astrophysics book. I showed her Libra, except she couldn't keep track of all the stars' names, so finally I pointed out the North Star. According to the film we saw in history, the Pilgrims used the North Star to help them find America. I told Elizabeth that since the North Star is so bright, you can always count on it to be your guide, even if you're lost.

"See," Elizabeth said, "you like the stars, and I like helping people." I was about to tell her again that I don't need help, but the truth is, sometimes I think that maybe I do.

# Do Not Resuscitate

"If you wear the layered skirt to the graduation you won't look so sickly," Mom said on the phone last night. Another one of my new privileges is that I get to go to David's eighth-grade graduation. Mom really wanted me to wear the layered skirt, but I told her I'd look fat in whatever she was planning on bringing over, so I didn't care what I'd wear. "What do you mean you think you're fat?" she asked. "Dr. Katz told us you're eating again." Then I explained how even though I'm getting fat, being hungry and dizzy all the time aren't worth it. "Besides," I said, "I'll probably have to be hungry a lot when I become a woman, so I might as well eat something before it's too late."

That's when I heard the crackly sound the phone makes whenever Mom sighs really hard and covers the phone with her hand. Finally Mom said, "She may be eating again, but she's still crazy. You try talking to her." Mom must think I'm deaf.

"Hi, honey!" Dad said when he got on the phone, which is a weird thing to say after someone else gets through calling you crazy. So I told Dad to tell Mom that she shouldn't bother bringing the layered skirt to the hospital, since I must be too crazy to go to the graduation. But before he could answer, I hung up, which I've never done before, but I've seen the ladies on Mom's soap operas do it all the time. Usually the lady gets all teary and screams, "You'll regret this!" and slams the phone down so hard it makes a little ringing sound. It wasn't dramatic like that when I hung up, but I was still glad I did it.

Mom came to the hospital anyway, though. After lunch today I heard her out in the hallway giving one of her phony kisses to Maureen, the arts and crafts lady. I'll bet Mom doesn't know it was Maureen's scissors I used to cut myself. If you want my opinion, Mom likes Maureen because her husband is a big Hollywood producer who knows Warren Beatty. When they're not talking about Warren Beatty and how hunky he looks in a football uniform with angel wings on, the other thing Mom likes to talk to Maureen about is her big diamond ring. Mom has one, too, and they're always holding their hands in front of each other's faces and comparing settings.

When Mom was finally done kissing Maureen, she came into my room and said, "I had a very nice discussion with Dr. Gold this morning." Like any conversation with Dr. Gold could possibly be nice. Then she said she was sorry I was feeling so hostile, and she understood my need to act out my issues of control, so she completely forgave me for hanging up on her last night. She should have just had Dr. Gold give her the lines through a hidden microphone, like on that *I Love Lucy* episode where Lucy has to pretend she knows Spanish so she has some Spanish guy telling her what to say. It was obvious Dr. Gold was teaching Mom that weird language he speaks. I mean, no one normal talks like that.

Then Mom took out some dresses and lipstick containers and said I should try everything on so we could figure out what I should wear for the graduation tomorrow. "I already told Dad I'm not going to the graduation," I said, but Mom answered, "Of course you are" and handed me a dress. "No, I'm not," I said, but then Mom opened up her big purse. I thought she might start crying and blowing her nose into a bunch of tissues, but instead she took out a crinkled piece of paper. "I'm not trying to control you," she said, except she was reading from the stupid piece of paper. "Yes, you are," I answered, but Mom looked back at the paper and said, "I'm sorry you feel that way." Except she didn't have any emotion or anything when she read her lines. Believe me, she'd never get a part on one of her sappy soap operas. I guess there was nothing else written on the paper after that, because then Mom got up and walked out of the room, but I could still smell her perfume. Mom always wears tons of this fancy perfume called Joy, which is funny, because she's always crying.

On the way out, Mom passed another mom who was sitting on the floor across the hallway. She was a lot younger than my mom, and I saw her sleeping in her baby's room for the past few nights. I heard Elizabeth call her Rita, and yesterday Rita cried a lot while Elizabeth hugged her. But this morning Rita wasn't just crying, she was making awful moaning noises. Then I saw a tiny bassinet go by with what looked like a lump of white sheets on top, and that's when I knew Rita probably wasn't a mom anymore. I figured the lump was Luther.

Luther came to the hospital a few days ago, and he was put two rooms over from me. I heard the doctors say that Luther was born without a cerebral cortex, which Doug told me is the thinking part of your brain. Doug explained that Luther was a vegetable, which meant he could live, sort of like a celery stalk lives, but he couldn't think the way people do. Then a few days ago Luther kept throwing up, so Rita brought him into the hospital. The doctors said he wouldn't make it, and they promised they'd do everything to keep him alive for as long as possible. But finally Rita told the doctors that Luther already suffered too much, and she didn't want them keeping him alive on machines anymore. That's when the Do Not Resuscitate code was ordered, and Luther became the DNR in room 4006. I saw it written in red on the memo board by the nurses station when Rita was crying and Elizabeth was hugging her. They were standing right next to me.

"Am I a bad mother?" Rita kept asking Elizabeth. Rita said that everyone thought she should keep Luther alive because he's her only son and she'll regret it if she lets him die without keeping him on the machines. But Elizabeth said that Rita was a great mom, because she cared more about Luther than herself. "I just don't want him to suffer anymore," Rita kept saying last night. "I'd rather suffer for him." Then Elizabeth left for her day off and Rita stayed and sang songs to Luther, but I guess he stopped breathing. That's when Rita started moaning.

Mom walked right past Rita and back into my room with some Q-tips and astringent she got from one of the nurses. Mom said a clean face and little color on my cheeks would make me feel better and also make me act less hostile. "You always feel good when you look good," she said. But when I wouldn't put on the blush, Mom kept telling me how I can't feel good on the inside if I don't look good on the outside. I told her that if you always feel good on the inside when you look good on the outside, then makeup would be able to cure all kinds of things that go wrong on the inside, even cancer. But Mom said she read in Dear Abby that the people with cancer who wear wigs and put a little blush on feel better than the ones who go around bald and pale. That's when I remembered the bald girl down the hall who has cancer. I kept praying Mom wouldn't go marching in there with her big bag of lip gloss.

Anyway, when I still wouldn't put on the makeup, Mom got out her script from Dr. Gold. "I understand your need for control," she said again, and she started putting all the makeup away into special plastic compartments in her purse. Mom tossed Dr. Gold's script in, too. Then she zipped up her purse and said, "I'm sorry if you don't want to, but you're going to have to go to the graduation. Your father and I have suffered enough . . ." but she didn't finish her sentence or anything. She was too busy looking for some tissues to wipe her tears with.

Mom was still crying when she walked by Rita again on her way out. Rita was crying, too, but at least she wasn't moaning anymore. She was just rocking back and forth and whispering something to herself. I really wished Elizabeth was here to hug her today, so I went out into the hallway to see if Brownie was around so she could hug Rita instead. But the minute I walked out my door, Rita looked up at me. It scared me at first, the way she looked at me. I wondered if she was thinking about how fat I look, but then she did the weirdest thing. She smiled this huge smile at me, even though tears were still pouring out of her eyes. I looked behind me to see if she was smiling at someone else, but I was the only one there.

So I was just standing there, and I wanted to tell Rita that I thought she did the right thing by getting the DNR. I wanted to say how great it was that Luther could finally stop suffering and go to heaven. But instead I went over and hugged Rita myself. Her body shook a lot, which kind of scared me, but at least I heard what she was whispering before. "Luther," she kept saying, and I felt her tears get my hair all wet. Then Rita stopped crying so much, and this time she whispered something else. "Thank you," she said. "You're a beautiful person." I couldn't believe she thought I was beautiful. I really wanted to say something nice back, but before I could think of anything, some doctor came by and took Rita away.

## Stick Figure

Mom came to the hospital after lunchtime to get me ready for the graduation. That's because yesterday Dr. Gold said he felt it would do me good to be around "real people" so I can work on my social skills. Like Dr. Gold knows anything about acting normal around real people. He spent the rest of the session trying to get me to talk about my big breakthrough, which he kept calling my "releasing of control." You could tell he thought he was a genius psychiatrist. He was so excited he even patted me on the head when he left, like I was a dog who did a neat trick in front of the neighbors. And Dr. Gold thinks *I* need practice with my social skills.

Anyway, today Mom brought over a bright, frilly print dress that looked like it came from the Caribbean. She probably saw ladies wearing them in those exotic travel books she gets a big kick out of. Mom also brought a blow-dryer and her big purse with all the little plastic makeup compartments. I told her that I wanted to wear the black jersey dress I had in the closet, the one that's baggy and comfortable and feels like a sweatshirt, but she said I'd look much nicer in the frilly dress.

After I put on the dress and Mom did my hair and makeup,

I went to go look in the mirror. That's another one of my new privileges: I get to look in a mirror that's bigger than the tiny bathroom one, but not full-length. Some privilege. Trust me, you would have puked if you saw me in that mirror. I had tons of blush on my cheeks and my hair was poufed out with all these big, loopy curls. The top of my dress was just like the one I once had for my Barbie doll, called Party Girl Barbie, except I didn't have big enough boobs to fill out the elastic part.

"I'm not wearing this," I said, but Mom told me I just couldn't see myself right because of my anorexia. "You have no objective sense of what's stylish anymore," she said. "Well, I don't like my hair either," I told her. "It sticks out too much." Then I grabbed a hairbrush to try to flatten it out, but Mom thinks anorexia means being unstylish *and* not liking big, loopy curls. "Fabulous, now you have anorexia of the hair," she sighed. "What'll it be next?" Then she said I didn't have any perspective, so she went to get some nurses to come look at me so I could hear how beautiful I look when I take the time to do something with myself.

A few minutes later, Elizabeth, Brownie, and two other nurses were standing around me and Mom in a half circle and smiling like mad. You could tell the nurses also thought I looked retarded, but they were probably too scared to say anything in front of Mom. "Doesn't she look lovely?" Mom asked, and everyone nodded and said how lovely I looked, even though I really looked like a very short clown. It was just like the story we read in English class called "The Emperor's New Clothes." Mom kept going on about how beautiful I can look if I'd just pay attention to my appearance, but then Elizabeth winked at me and said, "I think Lori always looks beautiful."

That's when I took off the frilly dress and went to the closet to pull out my baggy black jersey dress. I closed my eyes and threw the dress over my head, but when I opened them again, I saw that Mom's eyes were tearing up and she was dabbing them with a tissue to keep her mascara from running. The nurses left pretty quick after that. I swear, my parents scare everyone away.

After the nurses left, Mom asked me a bunch of questions. It's always trouble when Mom gets curious about things. Today she wanted to know why I'm purposely trying to be unique, and why I always wear black when all the girls my age are wearing celadon or fuchsia. Sometimes Mom gets stuck on one single point when she's mad at me, and I could tell she was about to get stuck on the color of my dress. She said that black is an inappropriate color to wear to a graduation ceremony, that black makes me look even more emaciated than I already am, and that dressing in black makes me look like I'm going to a funeral. But I still wouldn't change dresses. I really liked the black one a lot.

Then Mom did the weirdest thing. She sat down on my bed and said, "Come over here, honey," but I wasn't sure what she was getting at, so I didn't move. "I just want to give you a hug. You look like you need a hug." I looked around for one of Dr. Gold's scripts, but Mom's big purse was over on the couch and all she was holding in her hands was a giant round hairbrush. So I went over and sat on the bed and Mom gave me a hug. I could feel her tears getting my hair wet, just like Rita's did, but I didn't reach for any tissues. I just hugged Mom for a long time, then all of a sudden she let go.

That's when Mom put her face so close to mine she practically looked cross-eyed. She also grabbed my hand in her hand, the one with the big diamond ring. She was talking in the really soft voice she uses to help me fall asleep when I have a fever. "I'm only telling you this because I'm your mother," she whispered in the fever voice. "No one but your own mother would be this honest with you." Then Mom paused for a long time, like whatever she was about to say would be the secret that all mothers tell their daughters when they're old enough to know. I figured whatever Mom would say could change my entire life,

so I paid really close attention. Finally she said, "You look like
a stick figure in that dress. If you won't let me style your hair,
at least wear the nice dress. Your father and I will see a lot of
people we know there. Please, Lori, do it for me." I told Mom
that I don't look anything like a stick figure, but she got up
and brought me the frilly dress anyway. Then she looked like
she might cry again, so I changed into it and we left for the
graduation.

Mom loved David's graduation ceremony, probably because
there were so many cameras there. She was crying and making
Dad take pictures of her every second, even though *she* wasn't
the one graduating. Leslie and Lana were there because they
had older brothers graduating, too, but *they* weren't wearing
frilly Caribbean dresses. At least they were nice, though. They
came and sat with me, and Leslie invited me to her birthday
party, if I'm out of the hospital by then. After the ceremony, we
all went out to dinner at this fancy prime rib place where everyone at our school goes after graduation. But the funny thing is,
this time I was eating, and Leslie and Lana were on a diet. I ate
most of the prime rib, even though Leslie told me she'd never
eat anything that fattening anymore. She kept bragging about
how she lost two pounds.

After a while, my stomach starting hurting because I wasn't
used to eating so much in the hospital. I had to go to the bathroom pretty bad because of my stomach, but Mom stopped me
when I got up.

"Aren't you going to excuse yourself?" Mom asked, like we
were at the Queen of England's palace and I was supposed to
curtsy before I left. "Excuse me, I have to go to the bathroom,"
I said, but then Mom corrected me again. "It's called the
ladies' room," she explained. " 'Excuse me, I have to use the
ladies' room.' That's how a lady excuses herself." "Well, excuse

me for living," I answered, then I ran to the bathroom before Mom could give me another boring speech about being ladylike.

The first thing I saw when I walked into the bathroom was a really skinny girl who looked just like the pictures in Dr. Katz's book. Whoever decorated the ladies' bathroom was madly in love with mirrors, so I kept seeing the skinny girl everywhere. *She* was a stick figure. Then I noticed how the girl also had on an ugly frilly dress and lots of blush, but when I turned around to look, I was the only person in the bathroom. Except the girl couldn't be me because she was so skinny. I mean, it wasn't even possible, especially since I just ate all that prime rib. So I walked closer to the sink to get a better look, but the skinny legs in the mirror kept moving at the same time as mine. Then I smiled, and so did the mouth in the mirror. I even did five jumping jacks, and so did the body in the mirror. Finally I turned on the hot water and washed all that makeup off my face. That's when I knew for sure it was me. I couldn't believe it! I looked disgusting. I used to want to be a stick figure, but now I'm not so sure.

# Eggshells

As part of Dr. Gold's plan to help me act normal before I go home, today's bright idea was that Mom, Dad, and David would come and eat dinner with me. "Meals are highly charged events in your family," Dr. Gold said, like if you ate dinner at my house your hair would stand up and you'd get electrocuted. I told Dr. Gold that Mom and Dad love fancy French food and they'd never agree to eat in the hospital, but Dr. Gold told me that they'd bring in food from a restaurant, and I could pick which one.

I chose chicken tacos from a place in Hollywood called El Coyote. I used to love to bounce up and down in their big vinyl booths with David, so I asked why we couldn't just eat at the restaurant. That's when Dr. Gold gave me a lecture about how this was my "resocialization," and how he wanted part of my resocialization to happen "in a controlled environment." "I thought you wanted me to *stop* being so controlled!" I said, but Dr. Gold explained that this was a perfect example of why I need more resocialization.

· · ·

I could tell my family was here from the noise outside my room. Mom hugged and kissed every single nurse when she walked down the hall, like she was a bride and all the nurses were her wedding guests. Dad and David walked behind Mom and carried about ten bags of food. When Mom finally finished kissing everyone, we set up my tray table so I sat with David on my bed and Mom and Dad sat on the couch. I liked the bed because you could sort of bounce on it the way you could bounce in the booths at El Coyote, but then Mom gave Dad her nervous look, and Dad told me to stop. He said I could bounce all I wanted after they left.

So I stopped bouncing, but that didn't make Mom less nervous. I think she was more nervous pretending not to look at what I was eating. It was hard, though, because she didn't have much to do just sitting there. She wasn't eating very much herself because she already dumped her taco shells on Dad's plate. So she started talking about all the nice nurses and wondering why the single ones weren't married yet, and then Dad started talking about his tennis game, and David started talking about school being over. So I started talking about how I couldn't wait to come home, but then everyone got quiet all of a sudden, which almost *never* happens in my family. Everyone in my family usually screams at me.

The reason everyone stopped talking is because Mom is nervous about me coming home. Dad said that Mom's so nervous about it, they're planning on talking to the doctors again to make sure I'm really ready after just four weeks. "We need to come up with a plan so Mom doesn't feel like she's walking on eggshells with you," he said. I pictured Mom trying to walk on eggshells in those pumps she always wears with the skinny high heels. You could tell all the eggs would crack right open and there'd be yolk everywhere. "She's very nervous about your coming home so soon," Dad said again.

I told Dad not to worry because I already had a plan so Mom

wouldn't be so nervous. I said I'd be leaving to go to astrophysics school once I found one to apply to. "Astrophysics school?" Mom asked. "What are you talking about?" I told her that I had a long talk with Elizabeth, and I decided I either want to be an astrophysicist or a dancer when I get older. Mom thought a dancer would be a much better choice because then I'd get to wear those adorable leotards with the Danskin skirts. She probably has no idea what astrophysicists wear.

I figured Mom would be happy about me going away, but she thought she had an even better idea. "You could be a translator! Wouldn't you rather live in Paris and wear those chic tailored skirts and marry a romantic Frenchman? If I spoke French as beautifully as you do, that's what I'd do." I'll bet she would, too, but I don't want to live with a bunch of French people for the rest of my life. If they're anything like Monsieur Bordeaux, they'll keep yelling, *"Ecoutez!"* and making "r" sounds at you all day. "No, I want to be an astrophysicist," I said, but that made Mom open up her big purse and take out her compact. She got very interested in putting on her lipstick all of a sudden. It took a while, though, because first she lined her lips, then she put on more lipstick, and finally she smacked her lips together in front of the tiny mirror. She was still looking in the mirror when she said, "All of that therapy and you still have to be different." Then everyone looked away.

Dr. Gold's resocialization plan wasn't working, obviously, but I didn't say so because something was going on out in the hallway. It sounded like a party, and I figured one of the kids was probably leaving. I knew Mom and Dad would say I was rude if I asked to be excused early, but the minute I asked, everyone jumped up from the table and said what a great idea I had.

Out in the hallway, though, the nurses were crowded around Nora, who just came back to the hospital. They wanted to put Nora in "her" room, but someone else was in it, a kid named Eli who had his tonsils out. I was excited to see Nora again, but she didn't look very good. They had her connected to a bunch of machines, and she couldn't talk. The doctors wanted to take Nora to intensive care, but Nora's mom threw a fit and made the nurses move Eli so Nora could have her room back. That's when I remembered what Nora told me about wanting to die in that room, if she had to die in the hospital. I never thought she'd actually die before. I wanted to tell her that I was sorry for not talking to her after she told the nurses about the taxi, and that I know she was just trying to be a good friend. But I wasn't allowed to go near her. The nurses told Mom and Dad to take me away, so we went downstairs to the patio.

We stayed there for a long time, because Mom wanted to look in the gift shop windows and Dad wanted to look at the artwork on the walls. David found an old rubber ball on the patio and we played catch for a while. I couldn't stop thinking about Nora, though, so David came over and sat with me on a bench near the tiny trees. I guess he was trying to be nice again. Finally we asked Mom and Dad if we could go back upstairs, and that's when I found out Nora died. I couldn't believe it! All night I cried and kept thinking about how unfair it is that Nora died so young. Then I thought about how I once wanted to die, and how I could be dead right now, too. I mean, I figured *I* would be the one to die in the hospital, not Nora. But then something terrible popped into my head. I know it sounds awful to say, if you take it the wrong way. But the truth is, I was kind of happy I was wrong.

# You Can Never Be Too Rich or Too Thin

When I was packing to leave the hospital today, Dr. Gold came in to sign me out. "I want to assure you," he said, "that you'll have ample outside support when you leave." He also said I shouldn't worry about Mom thinking I'm not ready to go home, because he'll be seeing me three times a week in his office for the rest of the summer. He said he wanted to see me every day because he cares so much, but the insurance doesn't cover five times, and he couldn't possibly lower his fee. Thank God.

But the good news is, I'll get to see Elizabeth, too. She said that when I get settled at home, she'll go see *Grease* with me, because they do a lot of dancing in that movie. But I had to promise that I won't make fun of the actors until it's over, because she can't concentrate when people talk during the show. She even said she'll make fun of everyone with me, which is good, because Elizabeth is the only adult I know who has a good sense of humor. Most adults say things like, "You were skating on very *thin* ice there for a while, no pun intended," and think they're being hilarious.

. . .

I know this sounds funny to say, but even though everything's the same at home, something seems different. Not *unique* different, just *different* different. Mom, Dad, David, Maria, and even the birds are the same, so I guess I'm the one who's different. Like I don't feel like getting on the floor and doing a bunch of leg-lifts every second. I even threw away all the diet lists I was keeping for Chrissy and me. I don't know what's different exactly, but I'll bet Dr. Gold will ask me about it. You can count on that.

I'm not sure what I'll say when Dr. Gold asks, but maybe I'll tell him about this. After dinner tonight, I went back downstairs to get some water and I saw Mom in the kitchen. I thought she might be eating a chocolate chip cookie over the kitchen sink again, but instead she was busy organizing things. The minute I walked in, though, she slammed one of the drawers closed. You could tell she was hiding something. "What's in there?" I asked, but Mom said she was just putting some bar napkins away and it wasn't anything interesting. Whenever adults say that, it always means it's something *very* interesting. So I stayed in the den until Mom went upstairs, then I opened the drawer in the kitchen.

The bar napkins Mom was hiding were bright red, and they had pictures of little martini glasses all over the place. Then in the middle, there were huge colored letters that looked just like the writing on the Monster Cookie wrappers. "YOU CAN NEVER BE TOO RICH OR TOO THIN!" they said. Mom was probably worried I'd believe a bunch of bar napkins and start dieting again.

I didn't believe the bar napkins, obviously, but they kind of bugged me anyway. Because I think that maybe you *can* be too thin. And sometimes you can be too thin and not even know it, because you spend so much time listening to everyone talk about how ladies are supposed to diet, and how something's wrong with you if you aren't worried about being thin, too. It sounds like an incredibly stupid thing to believe, but after a while I guess even smart people start believing it. Even *I* did once.

Anyway, I didn't want Mom to know that I looked in the drawer, so I put the napkins back the way I found them. Then I decided to go upstairs and clean Chrissy's cage. But first I went into the service porch to get yesterday's newspaper to put on the bottom. It wasn't there, and I knew Dad would kill me if I ruined today's *Wall Street Journal*. That's when I came up with an idea. I figured I'd use the bar napkins instead. So now if you look in Chrissy's cage, you'll see "YOU CAN NEVER BE TOO RICH OR TOO THIN!" written all over the bottom, with little black dots covering most of the words.

So when Dr. Gold asks what's different, I'll tell him how I think saying you can never be too rich or too thin is a bunch of crap. I'll bet a million dollars he won't get the joke, but I'll probably say it anyway. Because I sort of do feel different now. And maybe what's different is that I kind of think there's nothing wrong with being different in the first place. I mean, it's possible, isn't it?

# Epilogue

I was almost thirty years old when I found my childhood diaries. I didn't plan on finding them, and I certainly didn't plan on publishing them. I found them only because one day it occurred to me that I might want to go to medical school (long story), so I went to my parents' house to look for my high school chemistry notes. It had been at least a decade since I'd been up in those shelves, and when I saw the diaries, buried behind years of schoolwork and class photos and report cards, I threw them in my bag. I figured they'd be some combination of painful and embarrassing, but mostly I thought they'd be amusing in a "Let's see what I was doing almost twenty years ago today" kind of way.

And at first the diaries *were* amusing—utterly naive one minute, startlingly perspicacious the next. Partly as revenge, I even read passages I liked to a friend who had been subjecting me to daily reports of the cute things her baby would do. But when I didn't pick up my phone for a week, I started getting worried messages: "Are you all right?" "Where have you been?" "Hey, let me know what you're doing."

What I was doing was reading my diaries, and by then I was

no longer amused. I was concerned. Because I realized that the girl in the diaries wasn't so different from the smart, witty, talented women I know today, women who say, "Do these jeans make me look fat?"; "I'll never fit into that bathing suit by June"; "I *have* to do the StairMaster this morning, my thighs are starting to get flabby"; "I'll have the Cobb salad, no cheese, no eggs, no meat, no avocado, and DRESSING ON THE SIDE." Often they sound more like my eleven-year-old self than I do, even though *I* was the one who had been anorexic. What, I wondered, is wrong with this picture?

We've all read the statistics: 50% of *fourth-grade* girls in the United States diet because they think they're too fat. An astounding number of women on college campuses have been diagnosed with eating disorders—and this doesn't include the so-called "normal" ones who are on constant diets, exercise compulsively, or routinely dislike what they see in the mirror if they don't look like the waif of the moment (Audrey Hepburn, Twiggy, Kate Moss before rehab, the new "it girl" Ally McBeal). But forget statistics for a minute: I could simply ask *you* your weight, and if you're a woman, my bet is that you have that figure branded in your mind along with your computer password and Social Security number; but if you're a man, it's more likely that you'll know within a ten-pound range what the scale said the last time you got on it.

I suppose that if a person is going to publish her diaries, she should have important insights to share. The intent in publishing mine, however, is more about asking questions than providing answers. Does being a woman have to be synonymous with being on a diet? Are offhand comments—about having thunder thighs, or being cursed with a slow metabolism, or saving desserts for the men, or needing to starve to fit into a dress —really harmless? I'm not saying that comments like these *make* a person anorexic, in the strict sense of the term. But I have to wonder, given the number of women who wake up each morning and determine their mood by standing sideways in front of the mirror *(thin: good day; not so thin: bad day, must begin diet)*, whether these attitudes have a more profound long-term influence than we give them credit for.

The line between between anorexia and normalcy can seem so blurred, in fact, that sometimes it's hard to tell if anorexia nervosa is a disorder wholly unto itself, or if it's partly an out-growth of society's generalized disorder. Did I have a disorder, or was my behavior the result of a larger disorder all around me? When *The New York Times, The Washington Post,* and *Newsweek* run stories on the increasing numbers of high-school- and college-age women flocking to plastic surgeons to be nipped or tucked or suctioned; when fashion models in the 1960s averaged 15 pounds lighter than American women of the same height, but those in the 1990s averaged *35* pounds lighter; when an ad for a new sitcom features a man who knows how to win a woman's heart—"Tell her she looks *too* thin"—*who or what is "disordered"?*

This distinction can be tricky, as I noticed not long ago at my cousin's bat mitzvah. My thirteen-year-old cousin—a top student, gifted creatively, enormously popular—aspires to become a pediatrician, and her friends are equally talented in their own right. But when I saw these girls standing in front of the mirror in the bathroom, their conversation centered around how "fat" they looked, how "gross" their "butts" were, or how they needed to go on a *different* diet. (It was assumed that they were *already* on some diet or another.) And no wonder. These girls' mothers were in the bathroom doing the same thing: talking about who had "let herself go" by "putting on a few pounds."

As I was leaving, I saw a group of thirteen-year-old boys walking into the bathroom next door. Can anyone imagine these boys studying their images in front of the mirror, utterly horrified by the shape of their stomachs or butts or thighs? Preposterous, right? So absurd, in fact, that Kellogg's used a similar concept in a recent television ad campaign. It featured men obsessing about the size of their thighs—a parody of what was supposed to represent a typical female conversation. The commercial gained instant national attention. For its piercing social commentary? Of course not. It was hailed for its hilarity.

When I was eleven, I asked my diary if it was possible to be different, to define oneself independent of waist size or breast size or whether or not one's personality meets a feminine ideal. Many eleven-year-old girls are still asking that question. The pressure to fit in (to a peer group, a bikini) can be enormous, particularly during adolescence, and those who aren't overly preoccupied with looking or acting in stereotypical ways—who don't go around chanting the mantra, "God, I *hate* my body"— are often considered to be "unique."

My diary may tell my story, but many questions I ask are not specific to me, or even to a bona fide anorexic. Young people's diaries can't help but chronicle certain universal experiences: "I think Bobby likes me"; "I got my math test back today"; "My parents are driving me crazy." Sometimes, though—"I was invited to Angela's big party, so I'm dieting as much as possible until Saturday"; "If my parents could afford it, I'd get liposuction so I can look thin when I meet new people in college"— they may unwittingly alert us to values that require further scrutiny. I hope that in some small way, the entries I've shared will help to do that.

# Acknowledgments

Many thanks to my agents, Jill Grinberg and Laurie Fox—experts at both cheerleading and dealmaking—for their unwavering support and for finding my manuscript an ideal home.

At Simon & Schuster, I was incredibly fortunate to work with Denise Roy—editor extraordinaire, fellow list gal, and discerning guide every step of the way. Not only does she have the patience of Mother Teresa, but she can keep more balls in the air than any juggler I know, and never drops a single one. She personifies grace under pressure. If Denise weren't an editor, she'd make a great emergency room doctor, or head of state. Laurie Chittenden's enormous enthusiasm got the ball rolling, and her judicious treatment of my words set me on the right path. I knew I was in good hands when she said right away that she liked more about *Star Wars* than Princess Leia's hairstyle. Brenda Copeland, Nicole Graev, and Tara Parsons somehow managed to make everything—probably more than I realize—run smoothly behind the scenes.

Sonja Grunden gets a great big "SON-JA!" for taking on both me and my book, for saying it like it is, and for being the most un-Hollywood exec in the biz.

The following people generously offered insightful feedback along the way: Mark Altman, Judy Budnitz, Nicholas de Wolff, Barron Ebenstein, Tim Farrington, Liz Fischer, Ted Frank, Jane Gutman, Lynn Harris, Samantha Hochman, Gregg Hurwitz, Gary Levine, Karen Loftus, Claire Lundberg, Eve Maremont, Rebecca Newman, Christine Roum, Kate Phillips, Sarah Saffian, Taylor Stephens, Dr. Michael Strober, and Anne Templeton.

Heartfelt gratitude to Carl Kugel, for telling me that I could be published, but mostly for telling me that I could *be;* and to The Group, for putting up with some of the same characteristics I had at eleven, and liking me despite them.

Most important, I thank my parents for buying me diaries as a child, and understanding my desire to share them as an adult.